THE WORM INSIDE THE ONION

Shirley Yanez

Copyright © 2023 Shirley Yanez

All rights reserved, including the right to reproduce this book, or portions thereof in any form. No part of this text may be reproduced, transmitted, downloaded, decompiled, reverse engineered, or stored, in any form or introduced into any information storage and retrieval system, in any form or by any means, whether electronic or mechanical without the express written permission of the author.

The views expressed in this work are solely those of the author and do not necessarily reflect the views of the publisher, and the publisher hereby disclaims any responsibility for them.

ISBN: 978-1-916820-52-4

CONTENTS

ACKNOWLEDGMENTS	vi
INTRODUCTION	1
CHAPTER ONE The undiscovered world within	5
CHAPTER TWO What are you hiding behind?	13
CHAPTER THREE You are worthy of serious attention	23
CHAPTER FOUR Stop pretending so much	38
CHAPTER FIVE Every regret is a lesson.	55
CHAPTER SIX Are you travelling the right path?	71
CHAPTER SEVEN Can we change or are we comfortable being uncomfortable?	86
CHAPTER EIGHT The unconscious objector	99
CHAPTER NINE Everything happens for a reason, or does it?	118
CHAPTER TEN A thought-provoking journey	131

ACKNOWLEDGMENTS

The Worm Inside The Onion is dedicated to Jenson, a curious ginger tom cat who belonged to my neighbor but decided to move in with me.

After I recently had to make the agonizing decision to put him to sleep, he was almost twenty years old, one hundred human years, I wrote this book.

Jenson was a fiercely independent thinker, with a driven, determined mind. I could always rely on him to wake me up in the early hours, just as my father did, religiously, when I was a girl, making sure I was never late for work.

I would also like to thank you for taking the time to buy this book and for being brave enough to begin your own journey of self-analysis.

It is not easy to admit you need help, but it is so much harder to suffer in silence.

Thank you, Kenton Hall, for editing this work.

INTRODUCTION

Imagine yourself as an onion with many layers. Layers you are going to peel again and again, until you reach the core of who you really are inside - the authentic you, buried deep. You are going to do this to discover why you might be struggling with the meaning of your life.

Peeling back each layer is a painful but liberating experience, that gently pushes you forward towards the psychological development of the real you. It's a difficult process that most of us never consider valuable or necessary; understanding the already wired workings of our brains is not always a priority.

In 2000, after losing millions overnight in the stock market crash, following years of climbing out of poverty to the top of the materialistic world, I crashed to the bottom, struggling to recover. But I didn't give up on myself. Then, in 2005, five years later, I had a near death experience, finding myself homeless, penniless, and dying in LA.

This time, given no choice but to give up on myself.

My whole world had collapsed around me. I found myself in the gutter of life with no power, no meaning and nowhere to hide. I was financially broke, broken and beyond repair.

Or at least that's what I believed, back then. We are all so busy rushing around, trying to be something or someone to please others or seek approval. We believe we have all the answers to all our problems and wait patiently for happiness and fulfillment to just arrive, often without doing any work on ourselves. Happiness is not something we can buy or rent. It does not come from external things. Trust me, I know. It is a concept. A state of mind that can only be acquired through self-reflection and complete honesty with yourself.

I want to help you recognize that you must see yourself from the inside to discover who you really are and what you really want. Always being brutally honest with yourself along the way. Your journey with self-analysis is about what is important to you, no one else. Looking closely at how you behave and why, understanding and being clear about how different things make you feel leads to a better understanding of your mind.

Is there separation between how you feel and how you react?

Are you able to distinguish your inner voice from your ego?

Are you comfortable spending time alone?

Are you following your own dream or one you have inherited?

Do you believe your happiness exists to represent the reason to live?

The basic goal of your life is to understand its meaning. This can only be achieved through gaining self-knowledge and self-respect. I want you to learn to look at yourself from the inside out, moving past how you currently see yourself or how others perceive you. This journey is about looking at you, both through your own eyes and those of others.

Who is that person you see when you look inside? Who is that person others see from the outside? Are you able to detect if what you see matches with who you believe you are? Do you believe everything you think? Are you comfortable changing your mind? Can you hold your hands up when you are proved wrong? These are all questions that lead you towards a better understanding of your behavior and how it is all related to your true values. This eventually becomes your character. Our thoughts become our words and our words become our actions; our actions become our behavior and our behavior becomes our character.

It is simple.

This bit anyway.

I managed to recover from my extraordinary downfall, make peace with my past mistakes, change my whole thought process, and reinvent myself. As the real me, lost beneath the fake materialistic life I had manufactured to find happiness. I fully understand now that the power of my authentic self will help me do anything to which I truly put my mind.

I am dyslexic but can write books. Today, I am successful once again, but with less focus on just making money. I am more productive, with purpose. I could never have imagined finding such power within when I was struggling to escape myself. Today I love myself, understand myself and can rely on myself without a shadow of doubt.

And I am now going to help you do the same through self-analysis. You are going to travel on your own onion peeling journey, discovering what lies dormant beneath, to uncover the true meaning to your life.

Empathy is the first value you will need to understand to begin this journey, particularly empathy for yourself. If you can become more empathetic, you'll be able to better understand yourself and how other people respond to you. Strengthening your character by being able to relate to your own life struggles, as well as those of others, helps you to begin the process of removing the outer layers of self-protection. These layers have formed over many years for many reasons. We never stop to really look beneath our pain for clues as to why our mental health could be suffering. We just carry on, until one day we either give up, burn out or convince ourselves that nothing can ever change.

You only get one shot at this extraordinary thing called life, yet many of us just strive and survive at a level below what we deserve, without ever reaching our full potential. The true meaning of life manifests once we can give something back to the world. It comes through creativity and self-expression, not through going through the motions until we drop dead.

Life is all about changing our minds, our attitudes, our perceptions, when faced with situations or circumstances we previously believed we could never change. In today's modern world, we seek happiness through materialism, often to the detriment of our biological needs, leading to dissatisfaction and a consequent inability to be satisfied. The result of this is an exponential increase in poor mental health. Sadly, many of us will never experience satisfaction or the meaning of life until we peel back our onion and release the worm of self-destruction.

CHAPTER ONE

The undiscovered world within

Digging out the worms from your onion – the unconscious flaws your mind has created that are now ruining everything you deserve in your life – must be done without judgement or fear. We all wear veils, social masks, false wrappings that cover as the persona we create, for self-protection.

We spend our lives from birth covering who we really are – adopting roles, following other people's rules, never conscious of the importance of being ourselves. The persona is the social mask we wear, often to fit in with society. Its formation can begin very early in life, as the pull of conformity causes us to identify most strongly with the social values of the masses, rejecting our own clashing personality traits. The big issue with this is that many people reach a point where they begin to believe they are the social mask they wear, cutting themselves off from ever connecting with the deeper realms of identity, the psyche. These layers and social masks represent but a sliver of the total personality of the individual self and can keep us trapped in the darkness of pretense, until we begin to malfunction and find ways to medicate our pain, rather than dealing with it.

This was me, sadly.

Over your lifetime, the pressure from commitments and responsibilities can build up and eventually affect your mental health in damaging ways. Enduring long periods of stress, life problems, mistakes, poor self-worth, and toxic adrenaline in our bodies, can eventually lead to many anxiety disorders, which then tip the balance in our emotions, creating poor mental health. It is so important that our conscious mind learns to acknowledge and make sense of all the thoughts, feelings and body sensations that arise from this stress. Behind the layers, built up over the years, at the core, you do discover the authentic self that existed before life presented you with its many trials and tribulations.

We are born perfect in terms of our energy and capacity for individual thought. Reliant on the information provided by our senses. We then spend the rest of our lives destroying this perfect start, constantly striving for perfection, often to please others, not ourselves. The core of your onion, under the layers of self-protection, is called your psyche. It houses your perfect clean energy, your light, your true character. A phenomenon involving the discharge of unique energy into the world to help attract all that is right for you - basically your own power. And this is the place we are going to travel back to on this journey of self-realization: the unconscious, unknown, often unrealized world within.

I am going to be with you every step of the way to teach you that everything you think becomes everything you are.

One reason why many of us lose connection with the psyche, the core, who we are, is often attributed to religion: one God, somewhere in the sky, who we believe is keeping tabs on our bad behavior and thoughts, causing us to repress elements of our personality. We end up striving for moral perfection, which hinders our natural development towards personal growth and maturity.

The more we strive for perfection outwardly, the more we fuel our dark side inwardly, losing control of how it manifests in our day-to-day lives.

The first step, the first layer you must remove towards self-improvement, is to let go of the idea of perfection and simply become more aware of the reality of your situation. We can only delude ourselves for so long before the manageable problems with which we struggle every day become ones we can no longer handle. Instead of facing our issues and problems head-on, in a mature way, we tend to ignore them or convince ourselves they are not important or affecting our mental health. We slowly cover the core of who we are with layers of pain, disappointment, fear, dread, anxiety, depression, and other mental health issues, until we end up miserable, depressed or in the gutter of life.

Many of us are unable to comprehend or explain why we feel lost, miserable, unfulfilled, or consistently unhappy with our lot. We just accept what we have and who we are because that's what we do and all we know. We go to school to gain knowledge, experience new worlds and ideas, to understand facts and figures…

But we never stop to truly understand ourselves, do we?

How many times have you asked yourself the question: what is the point? How many times have you wished you were dead? How many times have you made the same mistake over and over expecting a different result? That last question is often given as the definition of insanity. Why, after all, would we keep doing the same thing over and over, when it gives us nothing different? I know now, from experience, that learning new things about yourself and how much you need for your buried energy to be released, to be able to attract what is right for you, is the real secret to personal happiness. And learning new things in one area of our lives can trigger ideas in another, so curiosity and creative thinking go hand in hand.

When we are absorbed in where we are going, we can lose all sense of time and of ourselves. As our skill set improves, so do the challenges we face. Lifelong learning is not just about school, qualifications, career, relationships, marriage, death and satisfying self-centered needs. It is about understanding personal growth and how to function properly, without constantly malfunctioning or self-medicating for comfort.

This book, I hope, will take you on a journey of self-discovery, leading, in time, to wholeness: helping you step by step to peel back the layers of repressed thoughts and unconscious programming by others, until we reach the core of you were always meant to be.

Your natural energy sources.

Becoming a mature individual thinker without a mask to hide behind is not going to be an easy process. Self-mastery takes self-discipline and it requires undeniable inner strength to confidently peel off those protection layers holding you together like glue. I am hoping with my help and the new awareness you discover throughout this journey, that you will hopefully greatly improve your mind, your emotions, the choices you make, and your whole life.

Improving your life comes from improving your knowledge, but knowledge isn't just simply something that is collected by others or from facts proven by science. Developing self-knowledge is a completely personal thing and can be a very painful but liberating, insightful experience. I believe we could all benefit from therapy of some kind. By talking things out, we slowly clear out our internal blockages. But this can be an expensive investment for most, so all we are left with is self-analysis as an option.

I went on my own journey of self-discovery after reading the work of Carl Jung, which was enlightening but hard to follow, without doing some self-therapy first. Understanding anything new takes great study with plenty of failure. It helps you gain new perspective on the world around you. It trains your brain to better handle a wide range of life challenges. Knowledge not only fuels confidence but pushes you out of your comfort zone. So, we must always be proactive in learning more about how we function as human beings if we want to understand ourselves better and win the lottery of life.

Our physical body grows and develops without any conscious awareness on our part, but we are proactive in ensuring that we take care of it through what we eat and how we maintain it. Our psyche is the same: we may not be consciously aware it exists, but we can be proactive in reconnecting with it, to improve our mental health. By gaining insight into the workings of your unconscious hidden self, you will cast some light into the darkness, uncovering many enlightened lightbulb moments along the way. With every light you switch on, behind every layer of pain you peel off, there will be fresh insight into why you do the things you do, without even thinking.

Carl Jung wrote the following in 1921 and although it is complex, if you really think hard about what he is saying, it will make sense, as you begin to peel back your own unconscious layers.

"Everything of which I know, but of which I am not at the moment thinking; everything of which I was once conscious but have now forgotten; everything perceived by my senses, but not noted by my conscious mind; everything which, involuntarily and without paying attention to it, I feel, think, remember, want, and do; all the future things which are taking shape in me and will sometime come to consciousness; all this is the content of the unconscious." (Jung, 1921).

The worm inside the onion is all about explaining your own inherited, unconscious flaws and experiences across generations, which have created your personality today. The collective unconscious consists of pre-existent ideas and thoughts which can then surface in consciousness, in the form of your feelings, behaviors and sometimes your dreams.

I am going to try in the simplest way that I know to help you work on yourself and understand the difference between your thinking and your feelings. Thinking individuals make decisions based on logic and objective considerations, while 'feeling' individuals make decisions based on subjective, personal values. Carl Jung proposed that the goal of our psychological development is *individuation*. This is a process of becoming aware of oneself, integrating different aspects of personality, and realizing our inherent potential. It involves integrating the conscious and unconscious parts of our mind and reconciling our many inner contradictions.

By becoming more aware of who we are, we get to the core of all our issues and by doing this, we begin the lifelong process of self-realization and self-understanding, something very useful for good mental health.

If the idea of meeting your future self feels like meeting a stranger, don't worry. My job is to help you connect back, to get to know yourself better, so you can make healthier, wiser choices going forward. Remember that what is on the outside always reflects what is happening on the inside.

Self-abandonment, over your lifetime, to please others, has now left you a stranger to yourself. I know this is a head scramble but stick with me and be open because when your outside actions align with your inside values and feelings, you naturally experience less inner conflict. Just remember before we begin: you don't hesitate to see a doctor when you are feeling physically unwell, but you may presume psychological issues can only be resolved through praying for a miracle. I say, think of your mental health issues like cancer of your soul and clearly understand, this disease you have is exactly that, a form of unconscious dis-ease inside.

Everything that has come into your life to date, sadly, you have manifested unconsciously and has been created by the thoughts and beliefs you follow without question. Whatever is going on in your head, you are attracting back into your life. Every decision is a force of power.

You are not an accident waiting to happen, you are a powerful magnet. Once you know how to use your power, anything is possible.

I am living proof.

I honestly used to think I was invincible, untouchable, made of steel, but once I was forced into looking at my car crash life, I recognized my self-protection was hard, but my internal energy was just murky mush. I was missing three important things. Clear communication with myself, Curiosity to find out more about myself. And enjoyment beyond the fixes and fun that money can buy. The undiscovered world within me was never truly explored because I believed I knew everything about my feelings, my thoughts, and my behaviors.

I was wrong.

We must always be willing to engage in rigorous self-examination to discover important truths about ourselves, to gain a psychological advantage. The first step towards understanding the foundation of your conscious self is to look towards the unconscious strings being pulled without your knowledge.

CHAPTER TWO

What are you hiding behind?

What are you hiding behind?

Since the day you were born and potentially even before your birth, you have built up different layers into adolescence, to protect you from being vulnerable to the onslaught of pain and frustration this thing called life can bring. Even if you have amazing caregivers who nurture and protect you from all that is cruel and dangerous, you are not always safeguarded against the numbing of the authentic self. Our mental hardships are just obstacles that prevent our hearts meeting our minds, from being able to see our truth clearly. We must be aware that each of these obstacles can surface anytime and make us lose in the game of life; they will always create an internal struggle against what is needed to yield positive outcomes in all we do.

The development of all human beings, cognitive, emotional, intellectual, and social capability functions, happens gradually, from childhood through to old age. Human behavior is always influenced by our unconscious memories, thoughts, and urges, often without us having any control of it happening. That is a scary reality we must face, if we want to be happy.

There are many stages of human development, so this book is going to peel back all the layers to get to the core of who you really are. You are going to show up as yourself, vulnerable and all, so you can connect better with yourself and others in your life. It is so important to really understand what motivates you. This requires learning how to self-examine and be truly honest with yourself.

It also helps you to understand how to resist impulsive habits, developing more self-control with positive behaviors and feelings. Once you get to know who you really are behind those masks you wear, and what values guide you, you can more easily make better choices, including about the people with whom you surround yourself.

As you become more aware of your habits and patterns, you can better navigate your emotions, which then automatically improves your behavior. Getting to really know yourself allows you to begin to forgive yourself for anything you perceive as negative. You can commit to moving forward with self-compassion. So, let us begin to remove the first layer and understand how over time you have grown from your perfect energy, into a stranger in your own life.

Sound scary?

Well, let us be honest, it is no way near as scary as not having a clue what you are doing or why you are doing what you do.

The beginning of the creation of you starts with your infant development, growing from a baby into a toddler. In this stage we make our first human connections with other people, learn language, how to walk and experience our environment through our senses. It is a very important part of personal development because like a sponge, we soak up all the information, feelings, and experiences with which we are presented, without any protection against them. We are an open book without neurosis, hang-ups, masks, or a dark side. This period is all about safety and security, feeling comfortable with our surroundings and safe with those who care for us.

At this stage, we cry to gain attention. We are influenced by the atmosphere surrounding us and can feel tension and are sensitive to changes in tone of voice or other loud noises in our environment. This is also the time when we learn to trust the people who care for us in a consistent way. Not only do you learn to take your first steps at this stage, but you also take the initial steps towards becoming an independent thinker. Basically, this is your clean energy emerging into the world, supposedly without any interference or negativity from anything.

But we all know this is not possible because once we are out in the world, the world is a very scary, unmanageable chaotic place.

The language used by caregivers towards children in the first layer of development is critical for self-esteem later in life and will determine how they see themselves as adults. If your caregivers used phrases such as 'Don't make a mess again' instead of, 'Remember to pick up your toys' it is likely the child will feel told off, instead of clearing up becoming part of a routine they happily follow without question. We learn to problem solve. How caregivers communicate with children early on can weaken emotional relationships. If the child is made to feel unsure or unsafe about sharing concerns, their own ideas, or feelings, it can create distance, trust issues and fuel psychological problems, later in life.

The human personality develops as a composite of early conscious and unconscious childhood experiences. Any abuse, mental or physical, in this early stage of childhood development, can create a protective mechanism, leading to the splitting of the personality. The psyche is the place from where thoughts and emotions come. It is our self-regulating compass, striving to maintain energy balance between what others think and what we think as individuals. When the pain is associated with abuse or a lack of care, the self-protection mechanism can manifest in many ways and is the start of the development of layers.

It is not always abuse and neglect that creates protection layers. This can happen for many other reasons when caregivers unconsciously project their own issues. So, this first layer is all about the behavior we unconsciously use to separate ourselves from unpleasant events, actions and thoughts and is the beginning of the development of our personality traits. Anything that causes us stress or makes us feel unsafe, ends up becoming a self-protection layer we hide behind, which eventually creates internal anxiety.

By this point, you can hopefully begin to see that we are not just born to be molded, dictated to, or designed by caregivers. We are complex creatures with inner dynamics that must be understood and nurtured with great care, so we grow into functioning happy adults.

Coping with difficult situations and feelings when small, with no skills or experience to rely on, causes separation from threats, danger, unpleasant and unwanted feelings, such as guilt and shame. In simple terms, it is a way to take back conscious control and even at the start of our personality development, this happens naturally, without us realizing it.

It makes sense if you really think about it. As an adult, if you consciously lose control of unwanted, unpleasant thoughts and feelings, it stops you from reacting in calm ways to difficult situations, automatically bringing up negative emotions. As a young child, when you experience something that creates stress, the subconscious part of the mind monitors the situation naturally to see if it is going to escalate into harm. If it decides the situation is potentially going to emotionally harm you, it will react with a defense mechanism to help protect you.

As mature adults, a defense mechanism can be helpful now and again to cope with anxiety and emotional stress issues but as immature children, if used over prolonged periods, it can lead to long lasting problems. It can prevent the child from ever rationally facing their emotions or anxieties because instead, it blocks the child from ever facing the root cause in adulthood.

Instead of being able to face and deal with difficult emotions and stresses, the young defenseless child will unconsciously choose to hide them away in hope of forgetting they exist. In other words, they hide behind them, storing them dormant in the unconscious part of the mind, waiting for them to automatically pop out without any conscious ability to stop them.

Think now about how when you are angry or stressed, you can automatically react in the wrong way, projecting blame on others for no reason other than you are out of control and cannot help it. When anxiety turns to anger, it is because of an underlying fear about something else. If we are scared or worried about something, we often use anger unconsciously to feel like we are in control of the anxiety. These layers that slowly build from childhood become like security blankets, shielding us from painful experiences and protecting us from feeling vulnerable.

Some people who have experienced trauma in early life stages, when feeling threatened or anxious, unconsciously escape back to an early stage of development for comfort. It is hard to imagine that anyone would wish to return to trauma for comfort but if what you experienced in childhood is hidden in your unconscious, you are just following a pattern to which you have become accustomed and cannot consciously stop. Comfort is what you consciously believe makes you feel better in your trauma brain, which is in chaos.

So why do we seek comfort in chaos?

The truth is you don't know you are in chaos because you have become so used to it. Chaos is your comfort, which then creates your persona; the mask or layer allows you to operate outwardly, whilst inside unconsciously, you are a crumbling mess. You probably recognize this pattern if you are honest with yourself.

Your learned reactions as a child, become your well-worn mountain climb as an adult. It is often easier for you to go downhill, regardless of the effects and consequences, but getting back up there, i.e., working on yourself, is often very tricky because you feel more comfortable on the slide down.

What we experience as infants, molds who we become as adults. Our initial environmental experiences shape our future. Our emotional, physical, and cognitive maturity determines our behavior, therefore infants raised in caring and comforting surroundings tend to be more responsible, grounded adults.

This is not to say, however, that they never experience other types of self-protection and emotional scars.

As our world becomes more complex and the economic downturn pushes unwanted, unmanageable stress on those with children to care for, environments and circumstances become less secure and more chaotic. Addiction, divorce, and drug use are on the rise amongst poverty-stricken communities, meaning more children are experiencing unwanted trauma and distress in their early-stage development. This problem is manifested and exaggerated more because of social media, materialism, and an outdated education system.

We can learn to change our brains for better health - especially when we learn how we developed "trauma brain" in the first place. This is the key. The start and stop of the climb to a new habit is a great visualization technique for understanding how making change, feels. It is *not* easy.

Brain trauma is ingrained in people who survive dysfunctional families, so much so that it can become an unconscious part of our personality we cannot control. When you need comfort, it is often when you feel something is missing. You become uncomfortable because your needs are not being met and this results in stress, anxiety, or depression later in life. As an infant, when your needs are not met, this uncomfortable feeling becomes overwhelming and unconsciously you replace it with something else that's important, so you feel comforted once again.

You might also engage in activities that distract you from your sense of discomfort. It may not solve the problem or situation but might reset your emotional state, so you can feel comfort and a sense of inner calm. Not all of us have experienced early life adversity or trauma but what we are fed by caregivers and how we feel emotionally, at this early stage, becomes memories and reactions stored in the unconscious. Unconscious fear-related memories can remain totally hidden from the conscious mind, yet they still dramatically affect everyday behavior and emotions.

This is why it is so important to start peeling back the layers wrapped around your onion, returning to the start, to release and explore the unconscious memories potentially holding you back from growing up.

If your suppressed memories, traumatic or not, are not coaxed, by you, out of hiding and brought to the surface, they will lead to more debilitating psychological problems, such as depression, anxiety, or dissociative disorders. Facing the past, the pain and often the denial of what happened in your childhood, is never going to be easy because it is often hidden so deeply that you cannot reach it or even acknowledge it exists. You believe you had a great childhood, received everything you needed to become a centered adult, yet you have times when you cannot control your emotions and the reactions that follow. We all experience unexplained behaviors because we can pretend that we are happy, when in fact we are often miserable.

I found when I began the painful process of peeling back my onion to release my repressed memories and emotions, the best way to access unconscious memories came from tapping into and recalling the feelings on which I had become dependent.

By consciously returning to my unconscious brain, where the memory was initially encoded, I began to see patterns of emotions and feelings emerging. Basically, reliving the past through clear eyes, consciously without fear or judgment, was life changing. This was not an easy process because obviously I had powerful surges of anxiety that overwhelmed me. Through breathing deeply and meditation, however, I slowly began my own journey of self-analysis. It brought to the surface many hidden feelings that I had no idea even existed, let alone controlled how I conducted my life.

When we are highly aroused or engulfed in anxiety, the brain produces chemicals that create a state of homeostasis, our self-regulating process, which maintains stability while adjusting to conditions best for survival. If our buried unconscious memories are triggered by psychological perceived stress, fear, or anxiety, and not a real threat, our normal flight or fight response gets overrun. When you're faced with a perceived threat, your brain automatically thinks you are in danger because it is already programmed to think you are in a life-threatening situation and wants to keep you safe. This is a normal reaction we all experience.

It is vital that when you are to revisit the scene of the crime against your mind, you are fully prepared and able to control your unconscious ideas of perceived fear. You need to learn to relax through meditation and breathing, so that you feel safe and in control. After any traumatic event, even from the distant past, you may have an exaggerated stress response, which involves a recurrent pattern of unconscious reactions to the initial event. We are complicated creatures, so just imagining you can carry on struggling through it, without any internal work, is why you are feeling depressed and miserable or discontented with your life.

Peace and relaxation are the only ways to slow down your body's reactions and help clear your mind pathway for new thoughts and emotions to develop naturally. You can begin to recognize your fear-based unconscious memories, deeply buried in your brain, and monitor when they come to the surface into conscious awareness and under what circumstances. You can begin to discover what triggers the recollection of these unconscious memories that are hiding in your brain, those worms, your flaws. You can then begin to confront them with courage, instead of leaving them to continue to unconsciously affect your life.

Through meditation practice, you can find the space to prepare you for future traumatic situations that result in an overactive response. By regularly practicing activities that promote relaxation, you can begin to counteract the stress response with a relaxation response. Again, this is not a quick fix and takes work.

Let us go over simply what we have learned about our unconscious lack of control when we react emotionally. In the moment, our perception of the situation is altered. The emotional surge prevents us from seeing the situation for what it really is, and we automatically react instead. At this moment, there is no space for listening: our emotions and defenses unconsciously drive our behavior and there is nothing we can do to stop it.

It all just happens, automatically.

We can only truly know ourselves once we become conscious of ourselves. Becoming separated from your instinctive nature, the newborn authentic you, creates conflict between what is conscious and what is unconscious, between knowledge and faith, between nature and nurture.

The sole purpose of this journey is to shed some light in the darkness and begin the enlightening search for your undiscovered self.

CHAPTER THREE

You are worthy of serious attention

I have very little recollection of my own childhood, so for me to go backwards in time to find myself and what had led me to lose myself, I had to peel my onion from the outside in. Understanding what happened to me as a child, not from the perspective of others but from uncovering my unconscious memories, was a true journey of self-discovery. I thought I was operating perfectly normally with a relatively good childhood. It was only when I was forced by a life-changing experience that took me so far down, I could not get up, that I realized I was wrong.

Bringing unconscious memories to the surface, so they can be dealt with, resolved consciously and then released, begins by first understanding they exist. Then you are ready to begin the process. Slowing down and listening are essential in preventing emotional reactivity when stressed or in anxiety. Once we can learn to listen, we are attempting to take in what the other person is saying, and the main goal is to understand the message, without letting our own thoughts and emotions get in the way. This does not mean you have to be closed off to your emotions because that's impossible at this stage but learn to make a note of what triggers your negative feelings, so that you can reflect and examine them later, after the conversation.

Hopefully by now you can start to see what is at the core of your own onion self. The infant you, protected and hidden behind many layers of complicated processes, that can only be exposed through courage and determination. By wanting to protect yourself, you may have blocked those memories from your life.

It is my job to help guide you through the difficult process of reaching the younger part of yourself that is trapped inside, holding on for dear life to the terrible experiences it has gone through.

This younger self needs to be heard, processed, and then resolved but this can only be done successfully when you feel safe and secure, the hardest bit. We are all ready with a million excuses to not start making changes to how we live and take care of our mental health. We find it so difficult to jump off the exhausting merry-go-round and become grounded, happy and in control.

When was the last time you stopped in your tracks, took a big breath, and elevated beyond your own distractions, as an observer, to listen to your own mind and body?

Are you present in your own life?

Probably not for a long time. In truth, if ever.

We are all good at repeating what we do, when we do it and the reasons why we do it. We do what we do and forget to change things up by writing *new* life chapters. To feel safe and secure with any life changes, we must trust in ourselves, that we are mature adults capable of accepting responsibility for our own actions. We must take the first step to find out what triggers and wounds we feel, then step into the unknown to heal them with courage and determination, recognizing we will fail in the first instance. But that this is no big deal; we can always try again.

It is time to slowly remove the security blanket, the dummy and peel back the layers we have created, to stop us having to grow up and deal with our inherited issues once and for all. If we constantly repress our thoughts, which run counter to the extant moral system of our society, we will never reach those deeper layers in the psyche. The center of your awareness, your clean energy, which, when discovered, will substantially improve all aspects of your life.

A really good way to begin the process of self-development and the peeling back of your protective layers, is to no longer see yourself at the bottom, struggling to survive in a furious uncontrollable sea, but safe on higher ground looking down at yourself, drowning. This does not mean your struggle is being robbed of its reality but instead of being lost in it, you are somehow above it. The unconscious will always want to flow into consciousness to reach the core but, sadly, at the same time stops itself because it prefers to remain unconscious.

I guess because it is easier.

Nonetheless, it is a battle that you must win. Modern Man it would seem, would rather be preoccupied with materialism and other people's business, than in attempting to understand the elemental forces of his own psyche. Perhaps by now, you have a basic understanding of what could potentially be preventing you from facing your mental health head-on and why you have ended up hiding behind something, rather than shining your light. We have established that we are not born as preconditioned robots at the mercy of our caregivers but are individual thinkers who can change anything we wish.

If you are completely clogged up and riddled with neurosis, anxiety, depression, regrets, shame, and disappointment about your life choices, you are never going to benefit from the powerful energy sources you naturally possess inside. Your power and your light.

There are many explanations about what the psyche is; some are complicated but consensus points to the same thing: it is the place in your core where your deepest feelings hide. An invisible entity or energy which occupies your physical body. Your soul and, again this is open to interpretation, but for this book and your journey, we are going to see it as your power. We are going to use this power to help you turn on the lights to see your true feelings and behaviors.

There must surely be something more to us than just the biology of what's going on in our bodies and our brains. I like to follow the theories of Carl Jung because they make sense to me, and I have experienced incredible results myself doing so, following his path to the undiscovered self.

I also understand that if he lived today in this more complex world, his findings would be further advanced and even more interesting to follow.

The core, the whole self, including all our powerful potential is the organizing genius behind the personality and is responsible for bringing about the best adjustments to each stage that life circumstances allow. Once we can embrace wholeness and by this, I mean a standalone self-contained state of being undamaged, not broken or divided into parts, embracing sadness and happiness, loss, and gain, the conscious and unconscious, we become complete. We know who we are because our actions align with our words and our words align with our behaviors.

Once we can overcome the desperate search for perfection, which only keeps us locked in an imaginary world, rather than facing our reality, we are able to transcend beyond our perceived limitations.

We are going to begin your journey exactly as I travelled on my own and start by peeling back the outside layers, inward. This will give us a chance to see clearly, step by step, how what you are hiding behind is nothing more than years of self-doubt and accumulated baggage. You are eventually going to clearly see yourself truthfully and accept your limitations, as well as embrace your personal excellence, through rational feedback and self- reflection.

Let's begin.

The outside crusty layer of your onion appears a little dark. Old, not shiny. Or new, but battered and brown, limp and cracking. It looks like it is lived in and needs a makeover. Life has thrown so much at it, without much care from you.

It has weathered many storms and ended up looking identical to a million other onions stuffed in a box. You have become invisible, don't stand out from the crowd, and believe there is no other option but to be happy with your lot.

If this sounds like you, if you can relate, then it should be easy to immediately pull off the first layer because who wants to end up being described like that?

Removing the first layer won't really change that much in your life but it is the beginning of change. Think about it like having a clear out, decluttering the house and repainting the exterior, so it looks a bit fresher. You no longer wish to be one of a million, you want to be an individual thinker with your own mind, your own opinions, and your own unique footprints in the sand.

Because we are all unique, our life circumstances are also unique and, likewise, the psychological layers we enclose ourselves in are as personal as a fingerprint. This of course means that no one can really know how an individual's layers came to be or what they represent, without peeling them off, revealing the real issues lurking underneath. Peeling back your layers is an expression used in psychotherapy, as a metaphor, for what is going to happen during the amazing journey of self-discovery.

With my help, we are now going to take the necessary time to allow the other layers to peel back slowly. This will allow the hidden unconscious memories and feelings to flow up and emerge onto the surface of your mind.

You are now safe and secure, alone with this book, ready to begin your journey of self-awareness. This will help you to understand better what is driving you to feel and act in certain ways you can no longer control. We want to learn how to make better choices, feel empowered and not be held hostage anymore to the past, which now needs to go, never to return. Think about your onion as your self-awareness, with multiple layers, you are cautiously peeling back, to uncover your deepest motives, desires, and dark hidden truths.

You have let go of the first layer because it didn't look good enough for you. It was just the neglected dead skin you have allowed to act as your first impression to others. As we begin to peel back the next layers, you will learn to examine each one, by questioning yourself as to why you have allowed yourself to be lost and miserable, for so long.

Identifying your emotions and your feelings can be difficult because you are unaccustomed to doing it. The journey takes patience and practice. Just remember, through the years, you have been conditioned and taught to repress your emotions, often by caregivers, unconsciously giving you the wrong information or messages. Many emotions are also repressed because you believe them to be inappropriate, so we must also learn how to express these forbidden emotions, constructively without judgement. Since our emotions and thoughts are based on our values, a nonconstructive value can throw us into turmoil.

This is why it is vital to reveal your authentic core, as soon as possible, so you can rebuild your core values, construct your authentic character and by doing so, balance out your thoughts, emotions, and feelings.

Understanding self-awareness is the number one goal for us all to achieve through this book together. It is your ability to perceive and understand the things that make you an individual, including your own unique personality and unique goals you want to reach in your life.

The self, *you*, will become your only focus and attention from now on, until we reach your core and embrace your whole self.

So, to recap. Through research it is believed that as infants when we first start out in life, we do possess some self-awareness. We know we are separate beings. Then, a more complex awareness develops, around the age of one year, when we begin to move beyond our immediate senses.

Our self-awareness tends to take a back seat then, as we become more focused on following the life template: the roads we blindly follow, leading us to create masks and layers to conform and fit it. One's self-perception may become compromised over time, so we must pick it apart and decide what is true and what is made up.

Discovering how we perceive ourselves is often an enlightening journey on its own. For many, accepting the negative side of things is easy but it is more difficult to accept the good. A whole person will accept both equally as part of life's reality. To understand wholeness, we cannot any longer blame our circumstances, we must find comfort within the uncomfortable and not hide behind blame or addictions anymore.

It is so important that we identify how we automatically protect ourselves, when faced with overwhelming moments of disconnection with others. We must learn to let go of the tight grip we keep on the fantasy that we are in control of because it prevents us from embracing the true blessings of our reality.

We must learn to surrender.

There are many ways to do this but for me, is to always identify the areas of my life I am trying to control that are beyond me. Some things we just cannot control, like other people. We can only control ourselves.

Our journey together in this book is to learn to make some space in the mind, to receive only positive messages, when currently, there is no room for anything new. Once we have cleared the necessary emotional space, through peeling back the layers and surrendering ourselves to a higher level, we are left with enough space to then let in others. We can begin to treat our debilitating issues differently, not as problems or obstacles but as challenges we know we can now overcome. It is often quite common to feel more than one emotion at a time, so we can end up having feelings about our feelings and this keeps us stuck in a loop.

Our emotions need the space to flow if we are going to become unstuck and move forward but this is all about feeling safe and hopefully by now you are getting there.

My job is to provide a safe space for you to bypass your overwhelming feelings, so you can move forward and remove more layers. Once you have found this space, you will have created enough room for the suppressed emotion to flow; healing will follow.

I want to go back here to childhood and reconnect you to your younger self before we continue with more self-reflection. Now you know that during your childhood, your identity was formed by your caregivers, and you learned to see yourself through their eyes. To grow a secure positive sense of self, during this early development stage, we need a strong sense of approval and love from them, to help us develop a whole operating system, to navigate this thing called life.

If your childhood was dysfunctional and difficult, life in later years becomes a constant struggle to attain the perception of safety and security. The whole broken way in which we view ourselves and the world becomes cloudy, difficult to manage and causes us to malfunction. Self-awareness doesn't have anything to do with age. Some people have little self-awareness for their entire lives. I have worked with many people who have experienced adult growth spurts, later in life. The truth is that, if you never experience any kind of emotional pain when going through a growth spurt, what we are doing in the book together, then you are not actually growing or developing any self-awareness.

To truly embrace self-awareness, we need to take a long hard look in the mirror without the masks and then fully accept that all the things we have gone through or done in life, are our own responsibility to clean up and no one else's.

If we go through this life believing we are a fantastic person without any flaws, then we can assume we have little self-awareness. We have all behaved badly, made mistakes, blamed others for our life outcomes and hidden behind our huge egos. This is often why we end up miserable in old age. If you can learn to say to yourself in your meditation practice that you have behaved badly, made mistakes, blamed others but then take full accountability for it all, felt humiliated and embarrassed, then you are well on your way to removing the next layer. The load is getting lighter.

If you are able with sincerity and without judgement, feel these terrible, awful feelings, bought on by your poor choices, say you are sorry and commit to never repeating them, you are ready to start this journey. Unless you can do this, by being 100 percent willing to be truly honest with yourself and learn to navigate the negative emotions and feelings that emerge, as you face your flaws, you will never learn or grow beyond it.

Learning and maturity can often improve with age, but many people still choose to never experience becoming self-aware or devote enough time to self-development. This is often the reason we are unable to be honest with ourselves and unable to apply values that challenge our egos. We find it hard to have empathy without self-reflection. We are unable to forgive those who we believe hurt us in the past because we cannot walk in their shoes or understand their patterns and stories. As we travel the journey together and slowly remove the layers we have unconsciously collected along the way, we will look deeper at our egos and find ways to nurture forgiveness, not just for ourselves but for those we blame.

To conclude this chapter, we will put in place some relaxation practices to help prepare for removing the next protective layer. We are slowly no longer hiding away, are we? We are moving closer to our internal happiness goals without allowing the past to get in the way.

Make some daily time for self-reflection, through daily meditation practice, closely looking at yourself in the mirror. When you face yourself, look deep into your soul, beyond just your face and see more than just your mess and regrets. See hope and forgiveness.

Start a journal and make a daily entry, improving what you see and how you think about what you see. This truly helped me during my own self-development because as I began to read my thoughts, I noticed my patterns emerging and what triggered my emotions to emerge. I slowly began to see myself, outside of myself quite early in this process, which spurred me further on to peel back more layers. There are many ways to be present with yourself and your emotions, which, in turn, can help improve your self-awareness. Meditation practice allows you to look inside and reflect in safety on your life to date, enabling you to understand what is missing and what you need to do to improve your negative thoughts, confused emotions, and uncontrollable behaviors.

Start reflecting more about your choices, rather than blaming others because at the end of the day, what is past is gone and what is left is all you have. Analyze more of what has happened to you and why you are unable to grow as a human being. Only when you can do this truthfully will you see clearly where you can improve things. Start to track your habits and patterns and keep a running commentary of your life on paper. The more you follow your behavior, the more you can see your mistakes, improving your commitment to yourself more every day.

Write positive letters to yourself, once a week, and imagine you are telling someone from your past, how you feel. The results will speak for themselves, trust me. Start talking more to yourself and less to others about how you feel. Ask yourself questions and analyze the answers, then write down what you feel. Before you go into a new day, set yourself an intention and ask yourself what you want to gain from it. This will create a new trigger every time you do it and change the way you think about the future. Waking up your senses without self- judgment and taking them all in, noticing how you feel, as much as possible, will get you used to handling your negative emotions in peace.

Remember this always: feelings, thoughts and life experiences should be allowed to flow easily in and out of consciousness without a strong attachment to any of them. As complicated human beings, with unconscious flaws and engraved troubles, we tend to become too attached to the idea of ourselves. Once we can see ourselves as separate from other beings and the world, we see ourselves in a different light, as thinkers and doers, not sheep that follow blindly. This small change of seeing yourself as a separate entity makes you feel responsible for the here and now, how you feel and think, what you can achieve and how others perceive you. The problem right now is, you don't know who or what you are, but you will.

No matter how hard you try at the beginning of this journey, I can guarantee you will ultimately find yourself slipping back, every time you do your best to go in the opposite direction. It is inevitable because making changes that have crafted who you think you are, over many years, will not be easy to consciously erase, overnight. Rome was not built in a day! It won't happen for real, the change in you, until you understand the true nature of human experience and the power that awareness can bring into your life.

It will be unexpected and happen one day with ease and surrender. Hard to imagine right now but trust me, you will get there.

It will become crystal clear one day soon, when we reach inside and touch your core, your life is not about accumulating things, ignoring feelings, or wishing for unattainable miracles, without doing any work. It's about just simply being yourself and accepting yourself as you are. You must learn to embrace the madness that has become your life and learn to laugh at the mixed-up irrational thoughts and feelings, no longer allowing yourself to become attached. Let it come into your awareness, then let it go into the recycling bin, without being attached to any of it.

Self-discovery and taking back control of your life is about surrendering your past pain and allowing yourself to express whatever you are feeling in the moment. The more you do this, the more you will empower your subconscious to listen, then act on the new message you are planting in your brain.

I hope now you have understood that self-awareness is your new gateway to personal development, something that may have been hard for you to imagine tackling before.

I can tell you that this may not solve all your problems, but it will give you more choices. Our aim together is to get you connected with your higher self and how long this takes will solely depend on how much you are willing to open yourself up to what is right for you. We will talk more about your higher self as we get closer to understanding and elevating the old you. It is all about intuition and insight, making your life experience more meaningful and it is very exciting. Something to look forward to during these more difficult parts of letting it all go. It is a line of communication between your higher self and your awareness that determines what changes need to happen in your existing thoughts and inherited beliefs.

The more attention you learn to give to what you do and think, the more you can access higher consciousness, giving you more insight gained from self-improvement. We know now that if your mind is crammed full of noise, is busy, fearful, and blocked, it is not possible to think rationally, let alone connect with your higher self to gain clarity and wisdom. This once again just clarifies why your meditation practice must begin now at the start of the peeling process because engaging in the quietening down of the mind enables access to your inner wisdom, the core of who you are. The broader more intuitive part of you that has not yet emerged from the darkness within.

The curious paradox is that once you accept yourself as you are, then you can change.

I had an agonizing time for almost a year about wanting to change just before I was forced by circumstance, overnight, without mercy. I was stuck in the security of the familiar, even though I yearned for more. More than just money, success and superficial happiness purchased on a credit card. I wanted to pursue my passion, follow my purpose but I had no idea where to start. I was afraid of the unknown. My mind convinced me that making a change was unsafe, but my heart was empty in the knowledge I was not brave enough to follow my instincts.

Eventually my mind won the battle and I continued to follow the wrong path, which led to, on the one hand, my downfall but on the other hand, forced me to change everything. There was no room for fear or negative chatter in my mind. I had no choice but to start again and this turned out to be the massive miracle I needed to force me in a new direction.

So, the truth is simple. Once we can face the reality that life is not a walk in the park but often a very difficult struggle from childhood, we are somehow freer to move forward. Accepting the pain will come and go, until we deal with it. Not one of us can say we like pain, but it is not optional when it comes to facing yourself and your life choices. Always remember, we will make it worse through continued avoidance.

It was important to take you back to your childhood days to understand about trauma because whenever we experience it, our bodies naturally release all the necessary chemicals and hormones needed for our survival. Our stress hormones skyrocket, adrenaline kicks in and our bodies tense up. We become numb, run away, fight to the death or freeze. Think now about things that may have happened in your childhood that caused you to unconsciously experience such trauma and how this is likely to have damaged your ability to handle stress, as an adult. Just remember, we hold on to trauma as a reminder of how we have been hurt in the past, with the sole intention of protecting ourselves from being hurt again, in the future.

CHAPTER FOUR

Stop pretending so much

Be proud, the first layers are now off, as you recognize that what you present to the world externally represents what could be going on internally. You won't be feeling too bad right now, hopefully. All you have done is removed the dirty brown crusty outer skin, accumulated over the years, which has become normalized and built up unconsciously: childhood unconscious experiences that may be dictating your current feelings. These layers represent a lack of interest in how you see yourself because you don't know yourself.

Not the real you anyway. You might think you know yourself because how could you operate, build a life, or have even got to this point without knowing yourself? That was also a long chapter, but now we will accelerate our journey because you have a basic understanding of a very complex subject, and this should help you progress at a faster pace.

It is truly hard to face the next layers and rip them off because it involves you admitting, probably for the first time in your life, that, perhaps, every choice you have ever made, every path you have blindly followed, has been wrong. But by learning to express your own emotions in a healthy way and practicing active listening to your heart not your mind, you're contributing to the expansion of your own self-awareness.

This is a good thing.

By understanding the underlying cause of your negative thoughts and lack of interest in your mental well-being, you are getting closer to understanding yourself but not blaming yourself anymore. You may not even realize at this stage you are potentially unhappy or that you need to change who you have become, to be who you really are, behind your many masks. You may now wish to crawl back under that crusty old brown layer and forget all about why you started this journey in the first place. But let's be positive because I believe in you.

Self-therapy is not easy and bringing your repressed emotions and feelings to the surface can be extremely scary. After all, you have been comfortable being uncomfortable for years. You may have decided that there is nothing wrong with plodding along as you are, never making a change because your life is not that bad. But believe me, growth is our greatest reward when we are faced with struggle or risk.

There is no personal growth without struggle. All actions lead to the reward of a deeper recognition of our inner strength. You can continue to tell yourself negative lies about how you don't need to change but if you can somehow overcome this mental blockage, the reward you receive will be truly life changing. Don't even consider self-sabotage. Embrace the complexities of your unique nature by developing an understanding of who you are, warts and all. Stick with me and dream big as you transform from being a victim of your own thoughts into someone who is empowered to choose their own thoughts.

One of the most amazing things about your mind is that if you are willing to put in the work, you can change negative and automatic thinking patterns quite quickly. This will take consistent practice because most of us have spent years listening to noisy internal voices that often aren't kind or useful. Since our minds naturally gravitate toward our familiar automatic negative patterns, we must create a new pathway, that eventually leads to automatic positive thinking. Again, struggle is a *necessary* part of growth. And struggle is a natural part of life. Finding comfort in the discomfort of your life is now our goal and this means accepting we are broken but always open to being put back together.

Let's look at self-sabotaging here because this early part of self-analysis can bring up many excuses and negative self-doubt, its natural and happens to us all.

Self-sabotaging behaviors often stem from your limiting beliefs about your self-worth. You may fear success because you don't believe you deserve it. This mindset is you acting in a way that is predetermining failure. Who said you are not capable of doing anything you set your mind to do? What is the evidence to prove you will fail, when it comes to facing your life challenges? If you are telling yourself that you have tried many times before to change but have always failed, recognize that once you stop trying and give up, it's over.

Self-sabotage is your brain's way of trying to protect you from emotional pain. It's a pattern and all patterns can be changed; you just need new action steps to follow, and this is what we are doing in this book. Self-sabotage is often connected with our unconscious beliefs, and this is why overcoming them takes doing some deep work with a therapist, to help dig them out for more examination. We must ask our higher self, what is the reason for this self-sabotage? Where did this self-doubt originate? Who planted the seeds of doubt in the first place?

Let's assume there is a deep part of you that is trying to protect you and has your best interests at heart, but unfortunately is not aligned with your conscious state and is not giving you the happiness that you deserve. This is the main reason we must go deeper behind the protection layer of your onion, to find the hidden memories that are sabotaging your attempts to achieve certain things. By doing this, we often discover that we believe we are not worthy or deserve to be happy or successful. We find that we fear the unknown and are afraid we will fail. Again, we are more comfortable with being uncomfortable. These unfounded, unconscious beliefs, which see us moving away from our personal growth, are happening because they feel unpleasant to us. We want to run away from the pain, which results in self-sabotaging behaviors. These unconscious beliefs, thoughts and patterns are truly irrational, so we must somehow learn to identify what is triggering them and then take personal responsibly for clearing them out, once and for all.

Keep reenforcing that your irrational thoughts, feelings, and emotions are all outside of your awareness, working behind the scenes, against you. They are unconscious triggers that keep you believing you cannot change anything about your life. Our problems arise when our unconscious beliefs create patterns and negative habits of emotional reactions and self-sabotage. This is often why we procrastinate and repeat destructive behaviors, directing us to do things we don't want to do but cannot help doing. It's a viscous cycle, ultimately ruining your ability to remain centered and rational.

We have already established, mostly we create negative patterns in our early childhood, that don't serve us well as adults and this is where the inner voice and cruel critic starts to take over, unless we bring into our awareness, identify, and change it.

The way you talk to yourself in your mind plays a vital role in your wellbeing, so be kind and responsible with yourself, accepting nobody is perfect and life is about lessons learned from mistakes. There is always potential for growth and learning with every mistake you make, so why be so hard on yourself? Hopefully now we can return to the job in hand, and you are closer to understanding more about why you had doubts about your ability to stick this out or ever make a change. We are going to have many doubts throughout this journey of self-realization. Meticulously taking yourself apart, memory by memory, to rebuild your confidence and desire to discover the authentic you, will be a huge challenge. Understanding yourself, when you don't really know yourself, is a tough, long process but get ready, you will finally be free and happier.

We are going to continue to peel back this layer to tackle your ego now, which prevents you from learning from others, the main reason you may have flirted with the idea of giving this journey up. Your ego changes all the time and is just an illusion, you confidently hide behind. The self remains as it is. The ego is the consequence of your thoughts. When your mind talks and thinks about things that happen in your life, it produces an opinion.

This opinion, then produces a reaction or emotion, and this is when the ego automatically pops out from behind you, to protect or destroy you. If you can live without opinions, you will never see your ego again but that's not so easy just yet. Your ego is also your self-image. How you see yourself. So, we need it right now but can dilute its power later, with more understanding.

Always remember, your ego stops you listening to others because it is defensive.

We are not born with an ego; it usually develops through social conditioning, self-protection, and the construction of ways to defend ourselves, even when we are wrong. There are many layers to your ego. It is delusional to believe the ego can be fully destroyed through self-realization but by understanding it more, it can lose its power over you. This can be a messy process, but all will become obvious if you go with me to the end of this chapter. The lesson, as usual, is don't cling on to anything, be willing to go deeper and deeper into the truth of your authentic nature. Find that state of complete relaxation and let go. Understanding how your ego works will become clearer, as you go over your mistakes in your meditation practice. You will get to see how easy it is to convince yourself you are right, even when you know potentially, you are wrong.

The more I studied my own life mistakes, the more I realized that we don't really have a separate ego that leads us astray from the path to enlightenment or our true nature. I believe now it's a concept. A label of who we think we are. The desires and drives that make up the idea of who we are. When I looked closely at my own life experiences, to find the authentic me, all I could do was examine my thoughts, observations, and feelings. My own view of the situation and how I saw it. The truth was, my thoughts, emotions and even my observations continually changed, so this led to seeing clearly that I was not authentic or set in stone. I changed with the wind.

If my life experience was built on just one static thought and had been consistent throughout, I could assume I would stay the same, but this is not how life works. The thoughts I identify with change from moment to moment, depending on what I desire to achieve. My idea to be this one consistent self, with the same consistent thoughts and emotions, to help me pass over the cracks during my downfall, was just wishful thinking. How we see things is so subjective and clouded, especially when we try and visualize the past through our unconscious. It's always skewed in the way we are programmed to see it, and never open for change, without feeling pain.

When we see someone on television, someone beautiful we envy, we must remember that what we are seeing has been constructed in our minds, through many pixels, and is not reality. So, at the beginning of my own quest to find myself, through what I learned from books about the mind, all I could find was my ego. I then turned to my moral thinking, just because it made sense to see if what I had convinced my mind I followed to the book, was what I put into practice in my life. Whenever we feel guilt or develop a stronger moral belief, from the one we had before, we feel like the previous belief was a mistake because we believe we did wrong. But is this really attributed to the self, which we have already concluded is not consistent with thoughts or is it the ego over identifying with the desire of a particular moment? You may have told a lie to get what you want, then told another lie to get rid of it because it didn't produce the result you imagined, it would.

After battling with the idea of self and ego, it was impossible for me to continue to believe the self can be ultimately good and pure all the time because that would mean becoming a religious fanatic. This was not possible either because all religions in my opinion have different beliefs and standards of goodness with which I could not identify.

So basically, I have concluded, if the ego is squashed or we indulge in the assumption that it is ultimately a fixed good or bad entity, it can only result in more unnecessary conflict in the mind.

Just like the psyche, we should start to see the ego as an energy, which can flow in many directions and be useful or not so useful in our self-development journey. Your ego is the source of your values but don't assume it is your fixed self because your values can also change like the wind. It is a dynamic force. Your values in one moment may encounter conflict with those of another, so you might pretend you think one thing to please someone else, when inside you are just lying to yourself to keep the peace, be included, or liked.

On this journey, we are not looking for perfection or moral goodness, all we are doing is resetting your unconscious thoughts, so you can find a freer authentic you, hidden behind the layers. Even the most religious good chant that we should destroy the ego, rather than blending it as part of our thoughts and moral goodness. So, we need to replace our preoccupation of trying to become the perfect and good self, with conscious recognition, we do have an ego that is useful and necessary but needs to be observed and managed.

I am convinced most people fail when it comes to working themselves out because the complex understanding of the unknown is so bloody complicated that even the best minds cannot explain it properly. There are many interpretations for the ego, the self, the psyche, so I just think of them as powerful energies I need to become more than just flesh, blood, and bones. If energy can never be destroyed and is the driving force behind the power within, then it is something that remains alive long after our bodies die and that's for another book, another time!

Hiding our feelings or pretending we are ok when we are not, is not good for the soul or our mental health. Why is it so hard to ask for help when we feel down and depressed? We have all learned ways to hide those painful feelings we experience in the dark, alone, and often without understanding where they come from. We also know deep down inside, it is not good for us to have these feelings or never express them, so instead we just repress them, so they won't come out and blow our cover. We do this automatically to cover up feelings of shame or fear. Over the years we have learned to be liked through becoming people pleasers or learned to be fake, to fit in or be accepted.

How many times have you masked your truth? The unworthiness you feel inside with a fake positive pretense, just to be accepted by others. It works short-term because it allows us to operate, and often we do it automatically without question. Faking it, until we make it, is okay in small doses to, say, bag a job or overcome nerves. If it has become your whole personality, you must look deeper at how this potentially affects what is going on inside you. Is the belief you are doing this because people won't like you or criticize you, if you be yourself, then feel hurt and ashamed? These negative feelings of shame and unworthiness are unconscious thoughts that come through, from your inherited beliefs. Your mind telling you to be fake, to make up for believing, you're unworthy. When you closely examine this crazy behavior, it is clear, self-doubt comes from somewhere else because why would anyone choose to be fake, over being themselves?

Again, I say, surrender your preconceived thoughts and feelings. Let go of whatever is holding you back but remember, this is not easy as we have already established. It is necessary to always have some self-protection during great personal change but stop lying to yourself, to impress other people. Be confident you are good enough, strong enough and worthy enough.

For this part of the journey, we will see your ego as the voice that protects you from feeling lost, losing the value of all you have gained so far in your life and everything you connect to. You have felt valuable, gained positive reinforcement, and felt meaningful in the world because of the things you have achieved so far, even if you don't believe it, right now. This is what your ego is trying to protect, when your negative thoughts convince you of something different.

We have now established that self and ego are energies that must be free to flow and never become static or controlled by preconceived ideas and thoughts, often planted by others or circumstances, in your past. These energies are separate to individual thinking and self-realization because they are things explained by others, with many interpretations, depending on different beliefs. I am hoping to just get you to a place where you can be free of what you have been indoctrinated with as a child and begin to develop your own identity, as an independent thinker, with your own mind.

What a concept.

Can you imagine truly thinking for yourself, without self-doubt?

To do this successfully, helping you overcome your mental difficulties, takes recognizing your feelings, finding potential positivity from them, gently pushing you to maintain balance in your life. You can start to begin to recognize more meaningful experiences, apart from the dormant unconscious ones you have automatically come to identify with. In your next meditation session, choose a problem you are struggling with, then focus on it and investigate what you begin to sense in your body when you recall the whole of the problem. Give this sense you feel in your body, a word you can identify it with, then go back and forth with the sense you feel and the word you chose to describe it, to see if it is right. You may feel a sense of being afraid in your body and use the word fear to describe the feeling. Then when you go over the problem in your mind, you might discover the word fear or being afraid does not match or fit the problem you are encountering. If you can distinguish between what you are feeling in the moment and what your problem is, does not match, then you can recognize anxiety.

Critcal thinking is the skill of clear reasoning. When we put forward an argument or we try and justify our opinion, some reasoning is involved in this process.

It is the skill of ensuring the reasons we give to support any claim we make, does support it. It is also about being consciously able to spot the ways we argue with ourselves, that often do not fully support the conclusions we come to. We need awareness to become fully aware of our problems before we put any thoughts to them. Critical thinking skills are then needed to identify what unhelpful or unjustified assumptions are. We think we are feeling fear because of our problem, when in fact we discover, we have nothing to be afraid of and our thinking is totally irrational. It is so simple when you say it and see it but when it is happening, it is automatic, unstoppable, and uncontrollable, creating more anxiety, every time.

Recognizing that anxiety will take you over, when critical thinking is missing, is the key to understanding how to control it. To face up to all your inherited dogmas and irrational thoughts, critical thinking is a good place to start because it allows you to address your anxiety more rationally than you did before. You find reasoning behind the irrational.

Anxiety is often triggered by stress, whether from a major life event in the past or accumulated effects of everyday stressors. Everyone's anxiety is different, so it is hard to pinpoint where it comes from or what it is in general terms. It is different for everyone and triggered by many different things. When we begin to peel back our layers, often we discover we are triggered by something we have unconsciously endured, during our early years learning. Difficult experiences in childhood, adolescence or even adulthood, are a common trigger for accumulated anxiety. Going through stress or trauma when you are young is likely to have a huge impact on how you handle yourself in your everyday life as an adult. It can be extremely debilitating and be triggered by experiences that automatically take you back there without any conscious control from you.

Anxiety is a normal part of life, and everyone experiences it to some degree from time to time. It can be challenging to deal with and can seem overwhelming when it reaches the point where you lose control. If you experience extreme feelings of fear that are out of proportion to the actual threat, like irrational fear, avoiding the source or enduring it. You find yourself withdrawing from social situations, or isolating yourself, this will greatly affect your ability to function, and your mental health will always suffer. This inability to function is when we start to cover our problems, with many learned coping mechanisms, as we have already established.

We may begin to pretend we are something or someone we are not, so we can cope, or we may turn to something like alcohol to medicate the feelings away. This then becomes a pickled onion layer which trust me, is a whole other chapter to explain later in this book.

Anxiety typically will not go away on its own. It often grows worse over time. Many of the coping strategies that people use to decrease anxiety, such as avoidance, end up making the problem even worse. This is when we begin to mask our symptoms by avoiding situations or activities that might trigger our anxiety. Masking is the way in which we start to hide the authentic self. to gain greater social acceptance from others. The true cost of camouflaging your real personality and emotions because you feel like to are not good enough, can cause you to feel a great sense of loss, which then leads to more anxiety and potential bouts of dark unexplained depression.

One of the traps we can fall into in this life is pretending to be someone or something we are not, hiding our true selves because we are afraid of judgement or rejection by others. Creating a mask or in this case, a protective layer, as a coping mechanism to deal with feeling insecure, including our propensity for negative self-talk, often comes from low self-esteem. This then disconnects us from our intuitive senses. When we hide who we really are behind a layer or mask, we adopt a counterfeit persona and is very different from playing a different role now and again. It can have serious consequences for your mental health and your natural ability to function under stress.

Understanding all the many aspects of mental health problems is critical when trying to understand yourself. Fundamentally, we are all burdened with inherited anxieties and peculiarities we cannot always control. I cannot in this book pinpoint every problem every person has. All I am trying to help show you is how the many layers of negative experiences and circumstances have become trapped, diluting your powerful energy source, preventing you from becoming your true self. To be healthy and happy, we must learn to release this energy with complete faith, it will carry us through the difficult times we face, until we know how to cope better without falling to bits or pretending anymore.

This is a journey many of us need to travel because many of us have forgotten who we truly are, under years of just going through the motions of life to often not get very far.

We have been disguising ourselves for so long and in this process, we have ended up with lives we don't really like or even want anymore. We just go through the motions, until one day, we either totally malfunction, medicate, or die miserable.

Removing the layers and reaching the core may not change your existing life but it will set you free to explore how you managed to get there in the first place. If we have followed a life template, inherited from our caregivers, and created our existence, performing many different roles, without ever truly understanding who we really are, what we believe or truly desire for real, it is likely we are experiencing, some kind of mental health breakdown.

It is not easy to just say, I am going to be myself because being yourself is a lifetime journey of courage and self-discovery. Steeping out from behind your layers, your fear of not being good enough, takes hard work and fully accepting without doubt, we can improve ourselves through self-reflection and self-honesty.

Becoming an authentic person and telling yourself the truth is never an easy process because when we find the courage to be ourselves, especially in front of others, we feel exposed and vulnerable. We suddenly feel anxious and want to crawl back under a rock because we fear disapproval and rejection, but this again is irrational and not right. I remember when I had to confess to my family and friends that I had lost all my money, finding myself homeless, after being incredibly successful. As hard as it was, it was a great relief. I was surprised how vulnerable and authentic for the first time in my life, proved my actions were aligned with my values and desires, despite external pressures to conform socially. People close to me began to admire me and help me, way more than when I was pretending to be something I was not, to impress those who didn't even care.

Swimming against the tide to become my true self, confessing my mistakes, taking the blame, and owning my lack of concern for others, during my climb to the top, brought me back to earth. It pushed me right off the pretending conveyer belt. It was truly liberating and took away the unnecessary pressure, constantly clouding my mind. I remember writing a letter to myself before I told everyone the truth about my situation, and it went something like this. I am what I am today, as I stand here with nowhere to run or hide. I have no choice but to tell the truth now because I can no longer pretend all is ok.

They can see me without my mask. They can judge me if they wish but whatever they do to me now, it cannot be worse than what has already happened. I am at your mercy with no excuses, just a person who made bad choices and is now paying the price. I am to blame, no one else. I have forgiven myself, my past and anyone I ever blamed for my problems. I am sorry and I have learned to be humble, grateful with empathy.

In everyday life, we are all adrift, moving and mingling in the crowd, playing out different roles, faking it until we make it. If our identity is determined by other people's expectations, we end up falling into the trap of never knowing who we really are. For me, to break away from conformity and begin to think and live freely from the shackles of my massive life mistakes, allowed me for the first time in my life to realize, my full potential. My life and my own personal choices in the past had been one continuing improvisation. It was me performing in many roles to reach the top, regardless of what I was doing to my authentic soul. Breaking away from the self-inflicted straight jacket of such a narrow-minded existence, was the moment I found personal freedom and began to live my life in the real world. I had successfully survived the many blows life had battered me with and was grateful to be alive, much stronger than ever before. It is powerful, trust me, so powerful, I changed everything.

Once you can guide your emotions away from non-truths and shift them towards your reality, you begin to uncover your real purpose for being here. Within you somewhere there is a path to a better life, and you are authentic to the extent to which you follow it. I can now hear you all saying, it's all well and good for me to say give up the life you hate to be free to follow a new path to a better life, but what about money, commitments, surviving?

Of course, we all have financial commitments, responsibilities or perhaps we are just sentimental about what we cannot let go of because it is all we know. I was lucky, I had no choice but to follow a new path after losing everything, including almost my life. I can assure you without doubt, having travelled this path myself, you become freer than you imagine. You must just stop making excuses because forsaking your own freedom inhibits you from seeking the realization of who you really are and what you really need.

They say life can be understood better backwards and this is what we are doing by peeling back our layers. Once we have achieved this, your life will be about only living forward. If your past has pushed you out to sea without a life jacket, adrift from the person you long to be and the life you long to live, we will peel back the next layer in the next chapter. Looking further inwards and then back outwards, between the past and the present to help guide you back, to the safety of the shore.

Just always remember, your learned behaviors are not solid objects you can pick up and change without doing the work because they are anchored inside your unconscious inherited beliefs. For now, they are trapped but you are not. You are free to look beyond the layers of your accumulated beliefs and decide if they work for you or work against you.

You have been pretending for too long that you are okay, without ever stopping to reflect on the choices you live by, endure, or accept. I am not saying everyone can just walk away and never look back but if you truly want to be more than you believe you can be, you need to make changes in your mind and be real without expectations.

CHAPTER FIVE

Every regret is a lesson.

We will never live a regret-free life, but we can live a life that is not riddled with regrets, causing us to nip in and out of depression every time we are faced with our perceived beliefs. As we peel back this layer, we are going to look closely at our regrets. By the time your life onion is fully formed, it is likely, as you tear back the layers, regrets about all the things you have done or what has happened to you, will be causing unconscious distress. When we live with repressed emotions and become conscious of regrets we are forced to face, medicating the pain away often takes over, in some form of comfort. This can be drinking too much, eating too much, drug taking, shopping and many other pleasure-seeking habits we believe help us to cope. We become dependent on our addictions to mask the negative patterns, keeping us stuck, battling our pain inside.

We begin this chapter looking at what addiction is and why so many of us are hiding behind it, just to get by and function better throughout our lives.

From my own personal experience, the secret to life is to always use action to help discover the things that truly matter to you. Living life to the full authentically. Trying new things without fear of making mistakes. This is how we evolve and grow beyond our regrets. Regret is an incredibly painful emotion and is rooted in feelings of great disappointment, guilt, or remorse, often for the things that have happened in the past. It can have a profound and powerful influence over everything in your present world and cause you to automatically drift aimlessly into bouts of deep depression.

We have established already that our ego, if we let it, can prevent us from learning from others. Envying others can prevent us from focusing on ourselves. Anger prevents us from seeing things clearly. Ignorance prevents us from making good decisions. Fear prevents us from seizing new opportunities. Regret prevents us from facing our problems. It might be here that you convince yourself you are not addicted or using comfort to make you feel happy and fulfilled. It may work in the short-term but never truly lasts beyond the moment if you are totally honest. We can forget the pain when it is pushed deeper but never be free of the consequences doing this has on our mental health.

Regretting the things, we have done or something that has happened to us, immediately unconsciously plunges us back into the past, feeling helpless, like sinking into a swamp, we cannot escape. Our energy and our time are wasted and taken away from focusing on the present, the moment. The calm place where we can make important decisions and choices suddenly changes, when regret is all, we can think about.

Looking back in regret goes against the principles of life. The principle of moving forward and living in the present. The truth is, every life decision we have made may not have led us to the right choices, but we must never regret something that has taught us a valuable lesson. **This is where you must pull yourself back and reflect.** If you have convinced yourself, you have no regrets or have never made poor choices, you would be lying again.

Denial is a powerful part that goes towards the development of your self-protection layers, so we must look at this now. Every one of us carries around a set of beliefs about many different things. Start to think about these beliefs as a compass that directs you to how you have constructed your life. The choices you made and the emotional responses you have to these life choices. How do the things you believe become in fact, what you do believe?

We have already established we inherit some of our beliefs, which can slip in unnoticed but remain in place unconsciously, continuing to dictate our life choices, until we die. What if these beliefs are not true or have been passed on to you in error? Some of your beliefs are based on what everyone else believes, like the life template of events we all blindly follow, without much thought. We often follow everyone else and get married because if we don't, we feel like social outcasts. Some of our beliefs become our beliefs because not believing them leaves us empty, with no other options. This is the denial path. An emotional rejection of what we really want inside, to embrace blindly what others do and want for us, instead. This is when we are lying to ourselves, just to fit in and be accepted. I am sure you can relate if you are honest.

When we engage in denial, we are then forced to find ways to disguise the unconscious uncomfortable feelings inside, to help us to believe the opposite of what we know, is a fact. This is not something you always do consciously, so it takes a lot of honesty from you to dig deeper and be brutally honest with yourself. This kind of deep self-awareness teaches us some serious lessons. We will learn more about this later, as we remove more layers, getting closer to the authentic truth about who you are inside, without denial to hide behind.

But for now, ask yourself some difficult questions about how you have come to believe, what you believe. If you really do believe what you believe or just believe because you have been told to? Think about whether you are protecting your beliefs, even though they are not backed up with concrete evidence? Think about how your beliefs came about and why you maintain them, without ever questioning if they are right for you. We are all human, and we all make mistakes. We all have regrets in life but maybe it's time you begin to forgive yourself for yours. You don't want to remain stuck in the ignorance of your unconscious forces within because this is what drives you towards addictions and comfort seeking behaviors.

When it comes to regret, we don't have a healthy relationship with it because we are usually looking at it through the wrong lens. Most of the time, when we look back in reflection, we regret the choices we made without asking ourselves questions. We persecute ourselves by imagining what would have, could have been, had we just taken a different path. We regret what was in the past and although we understand it cannot be changed, we find ourselves dwelling on it instead, until we go crazy riddled with feelings of guilt or shame.

We begin to compare the choices we made to an ideal situation, that we then convince ourselves we should have followed, even though we have no concrete evidence of where this could have led us. We simply imagine it to be a better choice than the one we originally made. Can you see how you do this?

When I think about my own life, I regret the actions I didn't take, far more than the ones I did. We can all regret the places we didn't travel to or never having the courage to jump out of a plane, so regret stems from inaction, much more than that of action. This is why in my own journey, while I made many mistakes, I can now look back and simply say, I have no regrets. Of course, after everything I have learned by making many mistakes, if the opportunity did ever arrive to go backwards, I might change some things, but this is the beauty of life, you try, you make mistakes, you learn and you grow.

You must never allow your regrets to destroy your life because this keeps you trapped in the past, only masking your pain further, to function better. Once we have a disconnection from our higher self and we live with regrets, this can blindly lead us towards addiction behaviors, to comfort our suffering and stop us having to face our truth, denial again.

It can become a self-indulgent pastime, wallowing in self-pity, that eventually becomes a comforting crutch that one cannot survive or often walk without.

Addiction has no logic. It's a pleasure zone that runs the show. It develops because the brain disconnects eventually from all logic and reasoning. It's a loop mentality you find yourself trapped and tangled in, until it strangles you without mercy. The reward system in the brain takes over, we hit the pleasure button (substance of choice) and continue the habit until we die. Recovery can only happen when we interrupt this loop and force new pathways to form, to reconnect to our brain. Addiction is a disease in the brain that pushes you towards what you know and that is, getting high. It is an escape from reality and a place of comfort. It is all the addict knows from a routine they build for themselves. Not all of us are weak because there are situations that cause anyone of us to overindulge in comfort, escaping from our reality, now and again. This could be a death in the family, Losing a job. A relationship breaks up. A song you hear that takes you back to a painful memory. But with addiction, even with the consequences of overusing clear to the user, the brain becomes its own entity, intent on helping you die.

Harsh but true, sadly.

When we are stressed and anxious, we long to find a way to get rid of the feeling, so we look for an activity we find enjoyable to help us escape the anxiety. We find it helps and continue to do it regularly, as a pleasure reward. We can escape our troubles frequently by the chosen pleasurable activity, until one day it becomes an automatic addiction habit, we cannot live without. When we seek pleasure or a need to let loose and escape, our brain produces a chemical called dopamine and it is very addictive and soothing when you feel miserable. Our brains are hard-wired to seek behaviours that release dopamine in our reward system. When we are doing something, we believe is pleasurable, the brain releases lots of this chemical and so we feel better, then seek more and more of the feeling. This is why junk food, sugar and salt are all so addictive, especially if you are not that happy with your life and have little self-control.

Those of us who have some self-control over our brains and can become involved in other activities, which give an escape from stressful situations don't always become addicts or addicted to comfort.

But those who have little self-control, and this again is often down to early unconscious childhood trauma, continue to find pleasure from that chosen dopamine release activity, do eventually become addicted. The addiction kills the pain and is instinct driven, whether it be bulimia, obesity, alcoholism, drug addiction, sex addiction etcetera. They are all shame-based responses, rooted in resistance to pain and the addict becomes powerlessness over, even facing potential death. This is the warning just how dangerous never sorting your mind mess out, can eventually become.

The one human function, only you can perform, is that of self-empowerment. I can give you some food for thought, based on my own knowledge and I can potentially get you thinking more deeply, but the empowerment to change your life or your negative thinking, is a reflexive activity. This means, it is you and you alone who can initiate and sustain the power of self-determination. Any recovery begins, only when you begin to take responsibility for your own actions and your own life. Self-destruction is all about self- harm and self-harm is all about, control.

When we are engaging in any self-destructive behaviours, it is usually to be able to deal with anxiety, self-doubt, or shame. This cycle usually starts in adolescence, when we possess very few skills to help manage the stress, of how we are feeling, when overloaded with negative emotions. We feel anxious and like we just don't fit in. We want some control over how we feel, so we find destructive ways to find this control, like bulimic who secretly control what they eat and purge what they hate about themselves. The bad food behaviour gives them a false sense of control. The behaviour is impulsive and compulsive but never sorts out the real problem.

It can take many stages to break the unconscious cycle of your self-destructive behaviours, First, you have the precontemplation stage. This is when you consciously know deep down inside what you are doing is not good for your mental health but subconsciously you are trapped in your emotion's turmoil and negative thought cycle. Next, we reach the contemplation stage. We decide we must at least begin thinking about changing because we have lost control of ourselves and potentially have created other self-inflicted physical health issues. Now we must think about preparation and what needs to be done by us to get back on track to feeling happier and healthier.

The preparation stage then leads us to action. We take the steps to do what we say we will do and do not lose sight of the end game. Once you begin to act and take positive steps to walk away from the mental wreckage, it is all about maintenance, making sure you are on top of yourself, every second of every day. Always maintaining the power to stay in control. Finally, you reach the end because your negative patterns, your negative cycles, your emotional turmoil have all be changed into new positive healthy behaviours. You can consciously begin to rebuild your life an independent thinker, not a dependent addict.

Humanity's propensity for self-destruction is a massive problem in the modern world right now, with the near extinction of any spiritual guidance or updated therapy available. It is becoming a global emergency. When I listen to addicts in therapy sessions, especially those who are homeless they say, I know that if I want to live, I can never have another drink or drug again because my hunger is without limits. Many say this but still cannot stop the cycle, so they are slowly but surely, killing themselves. Many of the addicts also when you dig deeper into why they have allowed addiction to stop them functioning, talk of their regrets and disappointments in life.

Many have lost what was once a good life, through divorce or the loss of a good job. Quickly their circumstances spiralled down to the depths of despair before they had a chance to consciously step in and act, to stop it all happening. All addiction is basically a side effect of not being able to deal with overwhelming emotions. In my experience, as a free talk therapist, almost all the people I work with have repressed issues from childhood, such as physical, sexual, psychological abuse or a traumatic event. Addiction is the only way they can cope with the emotional burdens these kinds of early experiences bring on, later in life. Of course, this is not true for every addict, but it is a common thread. People with early childhood trauma get sick of trying to cope alone and then sick of feeling ashamed of themselves for having no self-control. No one chooses to be an addict; it really is just a way for people to cope better and get through life.

It is important to talk about addiction when we are pulling back the layers because it helps us to ask ourselves if we are using things for comfort. We can also maybe relate to why others become unable to control their behaviours, especially when stressed or suffering.

This journey is about developing our own self-acceptance. Our acceptance of our attributes, whether positive or negative, as well as accepting our authenticity and current values. Your life is what your thoughts make it. Although you might have convinced yourself you are free, many of us are confined in a mental prison we have created ourselves; we cannot escape from. I like to think back to my own mental prison before I let it all go, to find my authentic self in the rubble. I remember to well my own inner critic, who became my jailer holding the keys.

This inner critic, the voice telling me what a mess I had made of everything, became my worst enemy but thankfully it was only for a short time. I hated listening to a voice that was not mine, dictating to me that I was a loser, making me feel ashamed and depressed.

I fought hard to find ways to silence this voice by asking myself where it came from and who it was because in my conscious state, I would never be a loser. I had achieved so much, from so little. For me it was not connected to a traumatic childhood experience or inherited from caregivers, it was just this voice of great disappointment and personal regrets. My time in my mental prison was not based on a fictional story, it was based on the truth and that truth was often unexplainable and very confusing to me.

I had no idea how I had got to the place where I had lost control. It just happened over time without self-reflection. Facing myself was brutal, especially because my ego was massive. I had to find complete self-control when looking back over my mistakes and it was the most challenging time of my life. More challenging than anything you could possibly imagine. I accepted that all the mistakes I had made were mine and eventually forgave myself for making them, but the inner critic kept poking its noisy chatter into my meditation, so it took me quite a while to silence it. I didn't lead me to addiction because I have never sought pleasure from false comfort, even during chaotic times of stressful situations. I am lucky in that respect and without a messy childhood, I was able to strip myself of my layers quite quickly. I managed to find the space between the unkind thoughts about myself, the blaming of others and some dark thoughts about suicide.

In this space, those short periods of sanity and self-control, allowed me to basically get a grip and anchor myself away from my mental prison. I began looking out into the sunrise to find some light coming up from the darkness, providing me with the simple joy and beauty of nature.

It is a powerful thing to watch something greater than yourself, work perfectly without much effort and it made me ashamed for even thinking about suicide. But for those of you who have deep repressed memories, flowing in from childhood, often to gain approval, be liked, loved, or admired. Or those struggling with the constant strain to live up to the expectations of others, sadly down to learned helplessness, it may take you more time.

It is also important here that I address those of you who believe your behaviours are sometimes out of control, but you are convinced you can take back control, if you decide to. If you are overweight and the doctor has informed you, if you don't stop overindulging, you will potentially die or create other more complicated physical issues, and you refuse to listen, you are addicted. There is no other explanation because if potential death is not enough to shock you into submission, you have lost control. This is not an easy thing to face of course but it is the truth. I am not saying it is easy to just give up your comfort eating but you must wake up and discover why you are a prisoner to your own actions before it is too late. The same goes for those of you who are functioning alcoholics, the bottle of wine every night to wind down or forget.

This is just a plaster. Although you believe you are helping soothe matters inside your mind, soothing your pain away, the dangers from too much alcohol intake, are only going to induce other problems, like weight gain, diabetes or will eventually lead to addiction. Whatever you are doing to ease the dis-ease, you are likely to be destroying both your physical and mental health. The truth is, when it comes to you believing you get pleasure in seeking comfort, this is you in denial. it is more about escaping and dissociating yourself from the pain of emotional isolation. In short, we all crave deeply intimate dependable, empathetic relationships but addicts, have learned, through trauma, that others cannot be trusted to reliably meet their needs. When we seek pleasure or comfort from our addictions, unconsciously we learn to fear emotional vulnerability, so choose to unconsciously distance ourselves from ourselves and from others. We unconsciously turn to addictive substances or comfort seeking behaviours, as the only way to not feel our unmet, emotional needs. We are complicated creatures remember and would never consciously admit to relying on something, to be able to get through our lives.

The main objective of this journey remains the same, to learn to be happier and mentally healthier, regardless of our circumstances or past pain. We do this by accepting our automatic emotional reactions to past events, preceding our rational ability to interpret the situations we endured, from a much higher level of consciousness. We must learn to have a much broader perspective and openness to learn different responses, to the dark challenges we have faced, leaving us hopelessly unable to control our emotions. I understand how easy it sounds but again, it is you who must now be brave enough to take the plunge and begin your own journey towards more clarity about what you are truly capable of. You don't need a comfort crutch to help you walk, you need to hold your head high and be proud to be a survivor.

Your meditation practice is truly the path to escaping your mental torture because taking deep breaths becomes the bridge that connects your pain to your consciousness, which then connects your body to your thoughts in harmony. By observing the negative thoughts that pop in your mind, you can begin to see a pattern of things that reoccur and recognize what is causing you to feel anxious. Looking at regret and denial can be an extremely painful process, so learning how to breathe deeply through it all, is essential.

As part of any recovery, and I am not just talking about those with addiction issues but all mental health issues, or any self-development, come under the same umbrella: leaving behind the past to travel beyond it. This is why working on yourself and your life choices, removing each layer and looking beyond what you think you believe, eventually leads to your personal freedom and unique happiness path. We must begin to see our mental health as important, as our physical health. Amongst the minefield of defences employed by our ego, we will find many mechanisms, such as denial, delusions, projection, and isolation, all repressed, which play a huge role in how we think and behave. It is complex and hard to understand but hopefully I can keep it simple, so it makes some sense to you all.

Though out this journey we will move forward from our regrets because we are travelling backwards to discover why we have them. Why we might feel depressed or have a meaningless existence. We might have never even looked deeply within ourselves or acknowledged why we are feeling anxious or lost. We may believe we have no issues whatso ever, but everyone should at least take time out of a busy hectic existence, to self-examine and evaluate any unhealthy habits we have collected along the way, that do not serve us well. Self-sabotage can be caused by a range of factors, including loss, a sense of meaninglessness, or feeling a disconnection from our spiritual needs. We will look at depression more as we travel back but it is important to recognize here, it is not just about emotional symptoms or feeling lost in the dark. Depression is like a black cloud on a sunny day that can be triggered or just arrive and block out sunlight, within seconds. It is unexplainable, unmanageable, and totally debilitating. It can last for hours. It can last for days. It can last for months. It can become your greatest enemy. It can also lead to so many underlying issues, without us ever recognising, until it is too late.

Many people who suffer from depression live with chronic pain or other physical issues, so it is not always just about problems in the mind; it covers many other problems we face. We can take pills as a plaster to reduce the symptoms of physical pain to keep it at bay, just like we can medicate mental health problems with addictions. But the truth is that, and unfortunately isn't taught, most mental health issues arrive a result of blockages that can only be fully addressed on a deep spiritual level, to become fully healed. Most mind problems are learned behaviours that can be unlearned if we are prepared to rip off the plaster and do some uncomfortable work on ourselves.

Depending on how deep your personal issues are. How long they have been repressed is an indicator of how much work will need to be done, to move your mind beyond them. And ultimately, how long it will take to you to end the negative cycles trapped inside, once and for all. All mental health issues can be truly difficult to resolve, so we never approach any of it lightly. The main reason it is hard to fix our issues because by its very nature, mental health problems tend to prevent us from acting when action is needed. Not everyone has a perfect life. In fact, I don't believe it is possible to grow and be happy without facing and feeling some pain and discomfort.

Life is not an easy experience to manage, especially if you have been travelling headfirst, blindly into many different phases, without ever pressing the pause button every now and again to reflect. Finding the right balance between selflessness, selfishness, and self-care, is not easy for any of us and no one can remain completely selfless. Loving yourself is something you must learn sadly; it is not handed to you on a plate at birth. So, if you are still convinced at this point, you have no issues holding you back, you have no regrets and you completely believe in yourself and your life choices, stick with me, you might find out there is more to learn, as we dig deeper. No one is perfect.

The next layer we are peeling back, is all about finding out if we have travelled the right path for our authentic happiness or if we have been following the path of someone else's. We can all follow the conventional steps in life by joining the herd but there are always new paths to discover, even if you feel trapped and stuck with your lot right now. We must never stop learning, growing, or understanding who we are because once we do, it leads us to lose ourselves forever and that's not healthy or the route to happiness.

Your unconscious beliefs are always at the center of your emotions, of your thinking, and of your behaviours. All this can be changed but it will take more than just consciously telling yourself to change. The most effective change of your unconscious beliefs and the best way to approach action against them, is to develop a strong mindful observer perspective. Stand back from your mental chaos, develop some awareness, understanding your onion layers, your unconscious beliefs, can always be changed, by you. The main thing we have discovered, peeling back this pickled layer is that any emotional distraction that keeps you from an emotional connection to your authentic safe self is down to escapism.

CHAPTER SIX

Are you travelling the right path?

How do we know if we are on the right path in this life that we have created for ourselves? Or whether we have simply inherited it from those we trusted had our best interests at heart?

Have you ever questioned if you are on the right path? It usually happens when things begin to feel uncomfortable. A bit like a niggling itch you cannot stop scratching, driving you mad. It's not really that prominent in your thoughts but just keeps irritating you, every now and again. It may have crossed your mind that you have been pursuing a life that does not align with your identity or your values and hidden aspirations. Are you travelling on the path to where you want to go?

Asking yourself difficult questions about your life choices and being truthful with the answers, are the first steps to establishing why you often feel unconsciously, uncomfortable inside.

We have already established that life can be messy and challenging, often unclear, and this may have caused us to change the idea of who we are, to please others.

By peeling back this layer, we have already examined our regrets and accepted they exist, we are going to try and work out what happened to cause us to have our regrets, in the first place. When we make choices, often based on conforming and not because we have truly thought things through, our view of the situation is often obstructed by what is going on around us, making it hard to clearly see the bigger picture. We can get dragged into things without lifting our heads out of the sand, to check that where we are heading, leads in the right direction for our long-term happiness. Have you ever stopped to examine, if the life you have fallen into, is the life you really want? Have you ever found yourself dissatisfied with your life but cannot escape it, without blowing it up? Is your life carefully consciously constructed but not making sense or making you happy anymore? Are you leading a double life, rather than ending the miserable one you are stuck with?

All these questions are rarely contemplated because we are so tied in, trapped, and committed to seeing it through, even if it does kill us in the end. Life is full of twists and turns. Often, we just stumble into things without clearly thinking it through, just to please others or because we are desperate to be like everyone else.

When we are young, it is so easy to follow the same path as our caregivers, adopting their values and beliefs, instead of blazing our own unique trail in the sand. And sometimes we just make rash choices in the moment that don't stand the test of time. Most of our bad choices come from acting on our emotions, rather than reason or instinct. Often ending up as depressing regrets, we are then forced to live with. It is here where we must find some resilience to combine emotion and logic, so we can learn to admit when we are wrong and then consciously learn from our mistakes and hopefully change.

So why do we make the wrong choices and often remain committed to them, even when they have disastrous consequences for our mental well-being? Of course, this is a complex question to ask yourself but often, we have made the choice ourselves, so blaming something or someone else, is not possible. It is true once again though, most of our bad choices are based on emotion and not reason or instinct. Unfortunately, our strong unconscious emotions cloud our conscious thinking and makes us do things that are not always the smartest or best for our own happiness. We have already faced, we run to denial, lie to ourselves, and often pretend we are in control, when in fact, we are under the influence or seeking pleasure from comfort crutches.

If we make a mistake, we need to be able to admit we made a mistake and never let our ego prevent us from openly doing so because then things can heal, and we let it go. Once we say sorry and take personal responsibility. Doing this means, there is no room for regrets, later in life. Like I have said many times, there is so much to be learned from your mistakes. We are all guilty of making them. So what?

As you become more aware of your mistakes, you can then upgrade your abilities to think before you act, approaching a more realistic place of self-care. The truth always helps to release your stored emotions from the past so masking your mistakes because you want to be seen as perfect or people pleasing, no longer feels important.

It is probably true to say, no one has abused you more than you have abused yourself. This is a hard one to swallow but if you begin to think about all the bad choices you have made, for all the wrong reasons, you might get closer to understanding that which is now, hard to swallow. The truth is, if we never consciously take back control of our own powers, we will never discover the enlightened path that leads to who we are.

Remember, our emotional self-abuse is always hiding behind denial. The ego, cleverly without our awareness, conducting our stories and unconscious beliefs, like an unheard symphony.

Let's look more deeply here at your ego again because understanding it more, might just help you to see why you have made some bad choices and not been able to get yourself away from the consequences, that have followed. One of the main reasons why your ego is your enemy is because it hijacks you from your reality and stops you hearing feedback from others. Your ego can show up also in less obvious ways and can be very difficult to spot when it masquerades as selfishness and is driven by a desire, to be loved or appreciated. You may believe you want to change your life, to make things on the outside much better, however it will be much easier to do this once you are not in denial about your inner chaos. No changes are ever made on the outside if you are still full of pain and chaos, on the inside. Once you change your own story, you automatically change your emotions, which automatically change your thoughts and behaviours.

The truth remains the same throughout this journey of self-discovery. Self-awareness alone helps you to see many different elements of your own story, allowing change in how you feel about them. You cannot ever change what you cannot see. And you only truly see, when you look deep within yourself, beyond your ego and your unconscious beliefs.

Many of our bad choices and decisions occur because they feel more comfortable and are triggered automatically in our unconscious emotions, steering us in the wrong direction. Pretty much everything we do in this life is a trade-off. Your life choices become at a cost to you or become of a benefit to you.

Potentially, the choices you made in the beginning of your story, were of benefit to you in the moment but may now years later, come at a huge cost to your mental health. There are always two sides to every coin and the same goes for this life. To know pleasure, you must feel pain. Life is not a one-dimensional experience or perfect. You must accept unhappiness exists to replace it with happiness. You must go through hell, to truly get to know yourself. Hopefully your own hell is not as bad as thought, by now.

We cannot just strive for success without accepting sometimes we will fail. So, understanding there are many choices you must forgo, to find what is right for you long-term, is the key. We spend our whole lives decision-making, deciding what we can give up enjoying or do something else and these dilemmas are at the core of what we struggle with in everyday life. So many choices, benefits, and costs. When it comes to making good decisions, we must think about all the gains we will make, over all the losses we no longer fear.

If your ego is your enemy and your life discussions have left you in denial with regrets and now depression because you are stuck with all the consequences, at least you can start to face how you got to be so complicated. For those of you who suffer with being indecisive, recognize it is probably because you never bothered to find out what is important to you or what really matters to you. Bad decisions or never making any at all, is way easier than making good decisions and often. We often knowingly choose the wrong ones, over the right ones. Its life. Just think back to the bad decisions you have made yourself and I am sure you will find, they were made when you were an emotional mess, not thinking straight and clouded by your ego, your anger, your desires, or you're your personal pain.

Let's look more deeply here and understand what your ego is, once again. Like I said in an earlier chapter, I believe my ego is a concept and no longer my enemy because once you reach the higher self, you stop it from limiting your true potential. In psychology terms, the ego plays a crucial role in the psyche and helps form our self-concept. An essential part of our cognitive function. When you are on a spiritual path, basically when you are reaching your better self, the ego becomes an obstruction to enlightenment, basically it stops you from getting beyond your own self-critical thoughts.

If the ego is left to its own devices, it becomes that nagging negative voice inside your head that then becomes the source of worry, anxiety, stress, and suffering. A critical enemy that must be acknowledged, tamed, and transcended. Understanding how the ego works will help you to quieten down that voice in your mixed-up head, so it does not have such an impact on the decisions you consciously make, in the future. Your ego survival depends on it feeling important and will fight to the death to defend itself. It loves negative situations because then it has something to do or worry about. Even in happy times, it is still lurking in the background, always looking for something to cling on to and trick you into believing you are right, when often you are wrong.

It really does takes us away from living in the present, the moment because it forces us to believe we are what we think and cannot change. It keeps you trapped in your head, stopping you from enjoying your life. It has this nasty habit of making you compare yourself to others, instead of believing in yourself. It punishes us and can make us feel useless, which then affects our self-worth. We forget our self-worth is subjective and must never be compared to others because we are all unique.

When you begin working on yourself, so you are more in control of your emotions and behaviours that follow, you tend not to ever compare yourself to others. You start to learn to shift your conscious attention on yourself, to work on destroying your unconscious habits and that negative nasty lying voice stuck like a record, in your head.

Understanding your ego and making it an ally, not your enemy, helps you to manage those uncomfortable feelings you experience, when you feel your deeply hidden beliefs and assumptions, are challenged. Sadly, once you allow your ego to take charge of your thoughts and control your life, you will never find peace or happiness. Whenever I found myself having negative thoughts, I learned to turn to what I was grateful for, and this changed everything. I visualized my ego as the captured concept in the mental prison, and not me anymore. Like I said we need it, but it is not in charge of me. I am in control of it and this is what we call, being at peace.

I became conscious of my ego and its unkind tricks to get to know myself more spiritually but never took it for granted because it still operates in the unconscious, until that is unblocked.

So, although the ego plays a crucial role in how we function in the external world, it does not explain what makes us human. We are not the thoughts we have but instead we learn who we are from the awareness of what is behind the thoughts. The ego is like a muddy swamp that pulls you under, preventing you from adapting to new ideas and thoughts for your own survival. It is intent on surviving and does so by keeping you with the same narrative and emotional cycles. It is nourished by your lack of faith in yourself. If you give in to the ego, you just invest more faith in the very thing that is sucking out your positive energy, so your pain and anxiety, just gets stronger. You must truly become ruthless with an unwavering discipline to pull yourself out of the swamp and starve your ego to death. Consciously watching it lose its power over you, while you do it. Be ruthless for once when it comes to your ego.

I had to find an unbending intent when it came to challenging my own ego mind and as I got closer along my journey towards, my authentic self. I watched and felt my consciousness beginning to expand. I began to find the value behind compassion. I started to forgive myself. I found true acceptance for everything that had happened and stopped beating myself up.

I changed, over time. My relationship with my mind blossomed. I made peace with it all. It became my ally that worked for me and never again, against me.

Once we have completed this journey together and peeled back the layers, understanding that your past has created your future, where you find yourself now, you are going to be much freer and no longer an agitated worm, in your onion. You are going to learn to live more in the present and less in the past, which is hard to imagine right now, and not so easy to do but you are on your way. Your mind and it complex issues will always to some degree distract you and pull you back into the swamp. Hopefully by the end of this journey together, you will recognize, if you continue to let your thoughts work against you, it will be much harder to surrender and grow beyond the past.

I now believe, we are all here on the earth to transform ourselves and become more spiritually minded. How we get to this place depends on many things. It depends on the circumstances in which we are born and the choices we make, the people we meet and the paths we follow. Through this life, we have carved our own paths but unconsciously, often made some wrong turns along the way. Sometimes, we have been totally unprepared for what life has thrown at us, but this is all part of the process of life, as we have already established, earlier on this journey. Life is a series of lessons that move us slowly closer to discovering our unique purpose for being here. However, as we begin to peel back the layers, we start to see, we have allowed our regrets, ego-self, unconscious beliefs, denial, and pain, to inhibit the growth process. We have allowed our ego to be in charge and our denial to keep us from facing the mess we have unconsciously created for ourselves.

Not everyone will have the same level of mess to face but most of us have some issues holding us back from leaving the earth as better people. We must begin to see this life we have been given not as a chore to endure but as a wonderful opportunity to propel forward, stronger, and wiser people.

It might have occurred to you by now, you have never had your own voice or opinions heard by those closest to you. Being heard is a powerful but often overlooked opportunity. We want to feel valued and understood. It is something we all long for because being heard can be a life changing experience. It is often fear on both sides, that often prevents us from being heard. We don't always feel safe in sharing our deep inner thoughts because there is always the fear there will be no emotional support, which we need to promote trust, which then promotes personal growth.

Creating an atmosphere of acceptance is not always easy, especially when you want to talk about your feelings, but we must try and encourage deeper connections, to gain better insight. I am hoping by this stage in our journey, I have been able to show you at least a little how your mind works both spiritually and psychologically, often without any help from you. We are not there yet but well on the way now. In the next onion layer peeling chapters, I will gradually guide you towards personal realization and self-discovery, so you can understand more about your life experience as an insightful experience, not a complete disaster.

I will try and explain about the elements of you which go beyond your senses and your capacity to perceive your reality. We have all been so influenced, for too long, by family, friends, the media, and popular culture, which have led us to cultivate unhealthy choices, make bad decisions, adopting a negative outlook on life. Once we get to the place where you truly know who you are and where you are going, your life will be so much more worthwhile, and you will be able to free yourself from all that has kept you stuck, struggling in that swamp. It's not going to be easy, as I keep repeating, but I believe in you and know you can rise above any mistakes you have unconsciously made.

Just remember your negative beliefs live in your unconscious and it is hard for you to consciously be aware they exist and how much they are ruining your life. I want to help you find your calmer self, calmer mind and improve your overall well-being. It is a real challenge to find the strength and motivation towards owning your personal freedom. This is something you are not used to doing. If you begin to see change, as a battle, you are the general who understands compassion. How to be kind to yourself. How to forgive yourself and those around you. As you begin to fight for yourself, instead of focusing on fighting with others, you gain more confidence and clarity about what you need and not always, what you want.

I learned that to treat things that were going to be hard and painful, I needed to be gentle and willing to trust myself. In the beginning of my healing process, I had no idea how to be ruthless or disciplined, tackling my mind was something I had never even contemplated. So, I do understand how hard it is. To me, the idea of being, on one hand, kind and gentle and, on the other, brutal, and ruthless, seemed like a total contradiction but this all becomes clear once you find more awareness.

I knew how to be brutal in my business world, before it all collapsed, but being brutal about my mistakes, was a totally different challenge, all together.

The simple truth is, you can remain stuck believing you are miserable, and your life will never change because the pain won't go away or you can believe you are stepping up and fighting for the freedom, to travel beyond your pain, to finally be happy. You are much better and much braver than the false stories you tell yourself about how you feel, every time you are faced with a trigger or a problem, you believe is beyond you. Step up and stand out. Be proud and be positive. You only get one shot, so aim high and jump start your mind today.

I wonder how many of you can honestly admit, the choices you have made, leading to the paths you have followed, have been fruitful and exciting or just challenges you endure, without question? Do you honestly believe your life is a catalogue of carefully constructed, well thought out plans or something you have fallen into by chance? It is a really challenging experience to stop and examine our life choices because it is something we tend not to do. We make our beds and then we lie in them, often lying to ourselves, we are happy and satisfied. There is nothing wrong with this, it's what we do but sometimes what we do, is not always right for good mental health, like drinking to get through it or overeating, for comfort. Here in the UK right now, there is an obesity crisis with more than half the population suffering in silence or spending their lives surviving by taking medications. This cannot be down to just the fact that we are living longer. It must also be about how we are not taking care of our bodies or conscious of what we are putting into them. I have experienced myself, not often but sometimes, unconsciously eating a whole packet of biscuits, in front of the TV. I have drunk too many bottles of wines, to forget my troubles. I have turned to comfort when feeling down but I have never allowed this behaviour to become a crutch I cannot live without.

Why are we not more focused on looking at the bigger picture, over-believing we can have what we want, when we want, in the moment? Why do we overeat, drink too much, take medication, rather than change our lifestyle? Why do we walk around with our heads in the sand, rather than hold our heads up high?

This life is not easy, I accept that, especially if money is tight, poor choices have led to misery and convenience has become an addiction that we cannot live without.

I think back here now to my own childhood, which I will talk more about in the final chapter, but it was very different to today. I was born in the fifties, just after a brutal war and life was not about convenience, fast food, keeping up with the jones or looking outward for happiness. Life was about recovery, gratitude and making the best of the little you had. I don't remember there being any obesity crisis or lives lived on credit cards. We had what we had, and people pulled together to help those who had less. It was a community spirit. I always think back to this time, when I look at the mess that we find ourselves in today, as a world. We see so much war, pain, and poverty on the box, it has almost become normalized. We watch weather disasters around the globe, caused by climate change but find it hard to imagine that we are a huge part of the cause. We just keep going, being led by what we are fed and get through it all, as best we can. Often complaining, blaming, or pushing our opinions out into the world, often without the answers to back them up.

It is hard to make huge changes in anything when everyone has a different opinion. This is the main reason politicians never get it right. We all just shout louder, to be heard.

We spend our whole lives trying to sort out other people's problems or putting the world to right, yet we rarely have a good look at our own behaviours, problems, or choices, to see if we are doing the right thing. This all might prick your ego and make you feel I am generalizing. But all I am doing is trying to help you understand more about the meaning of your own life, posing questions intended to wake up your mind and motivate you to question your own life choices. It is no different to taking in your car in for an annual MOT, to keep it working perfectly, to get you around and about with ease. You would never put the wrong petrol in your car, would you? If you did, it would eventually breakdown. So, putting the wrong information in your mind, or the wrong fuel in your body, is no different.

Thinking is a wonderful thing because you begin to question why you do the things you do, often without thinking. Why would we ever not do this? We are not robots, are we? We have powers. We are made up of energies. We have choices. We are so lucky. We have it all. So, why are we hell bent on destroying it? The paths we follow in life really do need more thought going forward.

Often, when someone else points out something to us that is not useful or going to produce the right result, we may consciously know that they are potentially right, yet we cannot always admit it. Think about your boss giving you a good telling off for losing a deal you had not prepared for. You know he is furious with you before you face him, yet you cannot help yourself from fiercely defending your own poor choices. This is your ego at work, defending the vulnerable you, but you cannot win this argument. He will always win because you did not prepare for the deal, or the meeting with him. You are just winding up your boss and potentially, he will sack you.

The right thing to do here, would be to hold up your hands confidently but humbly, admit you were wrong, not prepared, and sorry. It won't happen again because you have learned a valuable lesson, thanks to him. Admitting when we are wrong, is not easy but it is the best way to protect yourself from an onslaught of abuse and always prevents you from losing in the game of life. We cannot remain lost and vulnerable inside like small children, if we want to find the path to peace and enlightenment, beyond our mind madness.

People may not always present the truth in the best way, but we must learn to take personal responsibility when we know we are wrong, over lying or trying to squirm our way out. Honesty is the best policy when it comes to creating positive mental health. Of course, nobody is perfect but working towards becoming a better human being, understanding the difference between illusion and reality, right from wrong and self-control from mental chaos, will keep you centered. Today, I prefer being somewhere in the middle of everything when it comes to my opinions. I am learning to be open and keep them to myself, as much as I can, and it has made things much easier. If I hear something that pricks my ego, makes we want to react or my blood begins to boil, I have learned to pull back, control my reaction, and wait for the right moment to step in.

It is not easy but the more I remain focused on my own life, my own path, my own future, the less I am interested in wasting my time winning fights, that have nothing to do with my behaviour. I oversee my thoughts, my actions, and my behaviours today. I am always open to be proved wrong or given food for thought, even open to change my mind, if it makes more sense to me and my life. I never people please. I only please myself, without hurting others.

CHAPTER SEVEN

Can we change or are we comfortable being uncomfortable?

Jump-starting your mind is not different from jump-starting your car. You just need some leads and some energy, to get you moving again. I have hopefully given you plenty of leads and now the energy bit comes from you.

How do you change?

This is the most popular question asked by anyone who finds themselves struggling with the unconscious objector, negative, automatic beliefs, and a frozen mindset. If you really think about this question in more detail, you will conclude, most of us already know deep down inside, we need to change but choose not to. So, why is this? It makes no sense. Changing anything that feels comfortable because it is all you know, quite frankly is impossible without either genuine desire or something happening that leaves you with no choice. This is what happened to me. I had it all. I was lucky, healthy, attractive, confident, full of life, ambitions, with the unwavering desire to escape my humble but relatively happy beginning. Life really is a lottery draw. You have no say in who your caregivers are or what circumstances you will be presented with when you arrive. You arrive to either endure or embrace what you inherit. It really is that simple. All down to the luck of the draw, sadly.

I got lucky in one sense because both my parents greeted me with open arms upon my arrival. Were they happy? Probably not but nevertheless, they had stuck it out and managed to create another life to add to the family and be responsible for. I had four siblings older than me when I arrived at Howard Road. The house was small, crammed with noise and often chaotic difficulties more to do more with poverty, not pain. We were poor but not starving, just surviving. I was a kind of miracle baby, potentially a mistake but never made to feel like one. In the fifties, life back then was so much simpler than it is today. No social media. No TV. No aspiration. No materialistic greed, just day to day survival and the odd thrip to the seaside in a crammed caravan, for a change of scenery. In terms of the luck of the draw, in the lottery of life, I did well, and it was all about timing.

My parents had not been that happy together before I arrived. There was a ten-year age gap between myself and my oldest sibling. When I pooped out into the world, blue eyed and smiling, everyone suddenly woke up again. They all had something positive, to bring it all back together. Although there were problems, family issues and sibling rivalry, bubbling under the cracks, I was pampered and shielded for the first eighteen months of my life. I was feed nothing but love, admiration and was given an almost star like start, to rival any other new baby, on the street.

I have little recollection of this time and I believe this is because I was too busy subconsciously enjoying the glory of being the center of attention. This made for a powerful start to my life because instead of being unconsciously infected by negative messages from those around me, I was collecting confidence in abundance, developing positive personality traits. The building blocks of my infant stage were solid, and kickstarted the extraordinary desire inside to grow and learn more about life. I loved myself and was a fiercely independent thinker, who knew exactly what she wanted. There was no unconscious objector lurking behind pain, pulling me back or putting me down.

Through the years into adolescence, I encountered some choppy waters and plenty of experiences both positive and negative, as anyone would normally do in life.

I was blessed with a baby sister and looked after by an older one. My parents divorced. My mother left us in the not always capable hands of my father. Not that he was unkind or uninterested, he just had few skills himself and worked too many hours, to properly support us. He was often missing, at work, so basically, I was left to my own devices, to discover many vices that eventually got me from A to B. I discovered early in my education that I was dyslexic. Although this was a brutal pill to swallow back then, in terms of how I was treated, my innate confidence kicked in, and I found new ways to be popular and prove myself. I became an entrepreneur at nine and a terrible substitute mother for my younger sister. I sold cigarettes and sweets, making me the most popular girl in the school. I was very good at this but at being a good mother, not so perfect. I did my best, as always, but I knew even back then, being a mother was not a job for me and never would be. I hated going to school; it caused me so much pain to be different.

It was impossible to motivate myself to go but the money I made was useful, so, I spent more and more time in detention or being chastised by an uptight, repressed, miserable head who hated me, than attending.

I went on to have many different relationships with the opposite sex but to be honest, I was always too strong and confident to be trapped in a mutual partnership, where I had to compromise and make sacrifices, just to make it work. I was headstrong, determined and not going to die in the same place I was born. I wanted more, so much more. More money, more power, more experiences, more than just following the herd and being satisfied with my lot. I was grandiose in my desires but not delusional in my capabilities and for this I will be forever grateful to those people who gave me life.

I did have moments of temporary insanity, during my long but extraordinary journey to the top of the world, where I was pulled back into the life template. Primarily because I imagined I might be missing a trick or two. There are no tricks. Travel that path and potentially you travel backwards to where it all began and nothing changes.

The risk and reward of being free and independent, with no ties or responsibilities to keep me trapped, always brought me back to my own reality: total domination on the top of the world.

I have to say here, although I worked tirelessly and hard for years, had short marriages, had affairs, probably hurt many people, I was kind and generous. But I never stopped to look back and reflect. I was living my life like a fast train on a straight narrow track, towards what I believed I needed, to make me a happy, fulfilled, accomplished, human-being. When I did finally reach my unwavering goal, I was sadly missing one very important thing: my authentic self.

I had spent so much time and energy focused on a narrow-minded vision, knocking anything that got in my way to one side, lying to myself to convince others I was selling what they wanted, I ended up a stranger to myself, in my perfect materialistic life.

What was happiness, after all? What did I like? How many true friends did I have? What would I do next? I had pretty much done everything money could buy. I reached middle age, rich, powerful, greedy, and lonely. With everything one would imagine would bring abundant happiness.

Imagine is the clue here because what you imagine very rarely matches your reality. I had already won the lottery as a child, but it wasn't enough for me. I strived for all the wrong things, clouding my gratitude, and compromising my core. My authentic self was now hidden so far beneath the layers, it was out of my reach. I had no idea who I was or what was important to me anymore beside the money and stuff. I was shallow, blind to the truth and quick to blame anyone else but myself.

I agonized for ages during the glory days of my huge success, often feeling so comfortable, yet so uncomfortable at the same time. I began to medicate away the lonely empty hours with drugs and alcohol, praying something would change.

Be careful what you wish for. Overnight, after making some fatal personal choices, while under the influence of some very mind-altering comfort blankets, I lost everything. The money, the security, the lifestyle, the possessions. My pride. My spirit and most importantly, my health.

If you are finding yourself wasting your own life, wishing you had more than you were given, you must pull away from this illusion, right now.

I am not saying, never strive for more but always remember, money will never make you happy, unless you are happy before you make it. And take it from me, I am now an expert in this field. Even if you are happy, money and stuff are still not the only things you need to be fulfilled and enlightened. I think about my own journey, like a game of snakes and ladders, you throw the dice then travel up or down the board to reach the end game. You either win or lose.

I lost the game of life but won in the end and this is a head mash because how can you lose but still win? After the extraordinary life changing experience of losing everything materially, overnight, I hadn't yet reached the bottom. I was close but still had unexpected blows to my fate, to endure. Almost homeless, broke, broken and stuck in a foreign land, without any safety net or family to untangle my mess, I discovered I was very sick, encountering a near death experience, without insurance, in a hospital I could not pay for. All that money, all that power, all that glory, yet I found myself praying for something money could never by, the miracle of my life. My near-death experience was like every other life event I had encountered throughout my journey. I was not fazed by it, just disappointed in myself for allowing it to happen.

I am sure by that point, after such devastating loss, I had already faced the end and if this was my time to leave, then I deserved it. I would take the punishment without fear and just pray that whatever was on the other side was better than what I had encountered to date. This might sound strange, but I remember clearly looking at my dead body, from outside of my body and seeing a shell of myself. The fake person I had become, not the real me. Is hard to explain such an incredible event because it happened so quickly and who knows, if it was an illusion, wishful thinking or just a magnificent dream. I can only go on what happened to me after this life changing event. The things that automatically changed me forever and realigned all my authentic values, with my future actions.

Once I returned home, to the place I knew I would never die in, where it all began, years before, to receive free healthcare, to save my life, I changed beyond belief. Not because I decided to change, I am not taking the credit for that bit, but because I had no choice. I consciously decided, once I was well again and put back together, I would see myself in middle age as a blank sheet of paper. On which I would write my next journey.

Just imagine being able to start all over again, after wiping the slate clean, vulnerable but not afraid because there is nowhere left to hide? It was fantastic and, so liberating. All my different layers inside my onion, from the crusty brown outer shell, through to the core of the infant me and beyond, all my flaws examined, faced, put to bed, forgotten. I can talk about it, even write about it now, to help others but it never causes me to feel anything other than, gratitude. I am here today a new person on a new journey. A freer person who knows how to live life to the full, without greed and glory, driving the bus.

Every day is a new day to learn something new and yes, the world is in a mess, but I don't waste my time anymore striving for perfection, having opinions about things out of my control or worrying about the future. I live in the moment, the present, following my values and making sure they always align with my behaviour. The blank piece of paper is nicely filling up with new ideas and purposeful things, that truly matter to me and make me happy.

I am still a confident, fabulous, free thinking, entrepreneur, just as I was as a young curious girl. Only she is no longer in charge. I have spiritually matured and accepted the rest of my time here is a journey and not, a destination.

I am truly at peace, with no unconscious objector holding me back. My onion is finally put back together, the worms are all out, with a shiny outer skin, I am proud to display for the world to see. Unfiltered, never fazed, always grateful and not looking outwardly for anything. All I need lives inside of me and is powerful, authentic and in control. I am sure I still make mistakes but nowhere near as many as I did before my life turned upside down. I am a survivor. It feels great to know there is nothing that will faze me around the corner anymore. There is nothing to fear and nothing I cannot handle, without falling to bits. I am strong. I am not invincible. I am full of awareness.

Without a huge life changing bolt of reality, that pushes you beyond your limits, surrendering all you believe is right, into everything that was wrong, is not easy. I would probably be an addicted crazy basket case now; had I not been almost taken out and forced to change myself. So, I do recognize how hard it is for you to change. Changing how you think, feel, and behave presents unimaginable challenges, unless you can somehow cultivate a relentless driving desire to do so. We must want to be thinner, richer, and healthier more than we want to be lazy, unhealthy, lost, constantly complaining, and blaming others for our failures.

Let's look at why we have potentially given up the desire to change and stick with change, until we eventually do change. Marketing campaigns on TV with big brand messages are being used right now to attract massive followers. Subconsciously presenting and peddling illusions to you, the consumer, through social media outlets. Those of us who are not easily equipped with a strong enough ability to think independently tend to give away their personal power to these outside influences, such as paid celebrities or group consciousness movements, marketing themselves as expert influencers.

Too many of us believe that expanding our consciousness, and reaching perfection can be achieved through this type of consumer life coaching, from self-proclaimed experts, who call themselves gurus. We are subconsciously told every day, how we can buy perfection and happiness, have fabulous fulfilling lives, if we buy in, never committing to do some deeper inner work on ourselves. We don't need to do that because what we buy will magically do it all for us.

I am not a celebrity guru or a social media influencer. I can tell you from a place of real-life experience, observing the unconscious, destructive, that the negative patterns of behaviour we struggle to deal with every day, will never be wiped away by a magic potion or pill.

It takes you being real with yourself. Separating your mind from what you think you want, based on the advice of others. Those of us who are border on being reliant on materialism for happiness, tend to have highly ambitious, competitive, personalities, focused only on self-gratification and often without the money to pay for it. We buy things we want but don't need, with money we don't have, just popped on a credit card we spend the rest of our days paying off. But in the end, we are paying mentally, through stress, for such a convenience-led lifestyle.

These unhealthy, unethical qualities, often compromise good behaviour, doing anything to accumulate the possessions we so desperately want.

This used to be me. I lost all connection to the authentic me, the real me. I became a stranger in my own life, always hiding behind masks, personas, fake identities, never dealing with my internal chaos and pain. Which in turn, festered and influenced my every move. As you now understand, I hope, I discovered through my life-changing experience that to heal and change we must always question our true nature. We must then take positive steps to align our lifestyle to the circumstances, where we feel a true connection.

By doing this we find acceptance and purpose, which comfortably leads us to experience much greater peace of mind, bringing more joy, than pain.

It truly doesn't matter where you are right now. By being brave enough to really look at your current circumstances, make some assessments about what needs changing, then you are taking part in your own life, not trying to compete with someone else's. If you can accept what you see in your own life, as it is, and continually focus on improving your higher qualities and attributes, I know for sure, anything is possible now. I did it myself and look where I am today.

Let's recap. To heal, we must always question our true authentic nature, regardless of how hard it seems. We must begin to align our lifestyle to the circumstances where we can feel a deep connection, acceptance, and purpose, without fear or shame. We must understand, by doing this, we will find peace and joy. It doesn't matter where we are right now, this can always change but it is better you do the changing before the choice gets taken out of your hands. Through being brave enough to look deeply at your own circumstances and making a clear assessment about where you are, you begin to accept what you see as it is, continually improving your values and behaviours.

There are no magic pills, potions, lotions, or wands that can sprinkle gold dust over your life. There are no get rich quick fixes, to magically sort out your finances. There are no illusions that life is just a bowl of cherries you can just keep eating, until you burst. Your life is what you make it and although this is a cliché, it is the most common-sense advice I can give you right now. Remember, they also say the truth will set you free, another cliché but I say to this one, ask yourself, free from what? Why are you trapped? How did it happen? How do you escape? You will find you are trapped in your own lies and to escape, you must know the truth, about who you really are.

Honesty is the best policy. I love a good cliché, and this is my favourite. How many people say this but never actually put it into practice in their own stories? What is honesty, when it comes to looking deeply at our lives and asking those difficult questions? The questions we avoid, for fear of having to face the answers. Ask no questions. Tell no lies. Keep pretending to be happy and you're in for an unpleasant surprise.

When looking over my own truth and being brutally honest about my path to self-destruction, I recognized the narratives in my mind were not really mine. My mind was always telling me something that kept me focused and driven but in doing this, it was telling me lies. I was eventually able to confess and differentiate between the desire to win and the lies that made me lose. This happened through self-awareness and trust in myself.

I had no choice but to stop participating in the lies my mind told me. In the end, this stopped all the emotional suffering because the truth did in this case, set me free. You must move towards the truth by yourself, continuing to practice being honest with yourself, outside of the lies in your mind. Do this as an observer and not someone pretending to be someone or something you are not, to please others.

Being comfortable being uncomfortable is not an oxymoron, like you might think. We have all become comfortable being uncomfortable and have just got so used to it, we never question it. To take the first step out of your own comfort zone, you must learn to feel comfortable doing what has always made you feel, uncomfortable.

You may not enjoy whatever discomfort you expose yourself to in the moment but by doing so, you will find complete contentment in your personal growth journey, in the long term. The seeds we sow today become the trees we admire and enjoy, later. We are evolutionary creatures and need to be challenged to feel discomfort sometimes, to find our happier selves. We have already established, too much comfort is bad for us. We are wired by our past to escape pain and seek comfort. If we don't have discomfort, we get bored being too comfortable, so seek more and more, to feel satisfied. But instead of becoming satisfied, with fewer problems, we lower our threshold for what we consider a problem, ending up with the same number of worries. Basically, we search for and see problems, even when we don't have any.

You are probably asking yourself right now, if being so uncomfortable is so good for me, why is it so hard to get out of my comfort zone? Why am I so afraid to just try something new, something unknown? Well now you know the answer to those questions. It is your unconscious internal triggers and negative feelings of stress or self-doubt, always distracting you away from what you are supposed to be doing.

Your internal unconscious distraction tactics, that are preventing you from facing discomfort, when attempting to venture out from your comfort zone, now needs to be faced with more curiosity and contempt. You are the key to your own problems, so unlock your mind, unravel the mess, and take that huge leap of faith, into the unknown. The worst that can happen is you fail but so what, you keep failing anyway, so what's the difference? The difference is, you are now trying and no longer lying to yourself.

Learning to be comfortable being uncomfortable, means that you are finally getting used to being in different situations that are outside of your comfort zone, and this will open, so many new feelings of empowerment. You cannot live the rest of your life in fear of failure, disguising your shame with more pain. To grow and learn you must work harder at believing in yourself. If you want to learn to drive, you must take lessons. If you want to be physically stronger, you build muscles and if you want to get out of your comfort zone, you must face new situations and challenges without convincing yourself, you will fail.

CHAPTER EIGHT

The unconscious objector

When you really think hard about the lottery of your own life, now I have spilled my guts about mine, it should be much easier for you to face this final layer because we are close to your core now. Unfortunately peeling back this layer might be truly uncomfortable and take some extra courage. We are going try and meet your younger self, before it got buried under life and became a little lost worm. Understanding maturity and spiritual enlightenment, basically growing as an independent thinker, is all about letting go of the past, to see the future. A future you deserve and not something you endure without questioning or changing what is right for you.

We have established, much of our personality is set in stone from our childhood but what you are like, isn't really you. Once we can see our childhood selves much clearer, we begin to see the life path we have followed and our character much clearer. Were you the same person at three that you are today at twenty-three or have you substantially changed? Are you disconnected from your childhood or are you still trapped in it? We have already established your past does not have to determine your future if you can learn to live only in the present moment. If you remain trapped in the past, you will never evolve to embrace all you are in the present. You will never uncover your true potential and that would be a waste of your life.

Let's first examine what the unconscious objector is, the title of this chapter. Examining everything we have learned on this journey together, hopefully now you will conclude, all that is driving your patterns, habits, negative thinking, behaviours, addictions, mental health issues, lies and regrets are unconscious and not your fault They happen without you consciously being aware they even exist. This means, we do things automatically we don't feel comfortable about, without ever understanding why we keep doing them. Remember, the definition of insanity is to repeat the same behaviour and expect a different result. When you really think more about this sentence more, you start to see. your mind is the one who is insane, and not you.

Our fears and anxiety dictate how we feel, especially when we are faced with stressful situations. As much as we may hate this automatic response, we cannot control it or always clearly understand where it comes from. It is like we are pretending with everything we have inside to be mature adults, captains of our own ships, with no clue how to operate the engine. We are often lost, navigating the choppy waters of life with no direction or idea where we are headed. We just get through it the best we can, and hope things will improve.

So, what is going on and why do we have little self-control, when frozen solid by those feelings of anxiety or fear, we cannot explain? By travelling back through many self-protecting layers, we have established many things about ourselves and why we are stuck. The truth is, when we are lying to ourselves, pretending we are happy, all is good and we have got to where we are without thinking, it is no wonder we become like deer in the headlights, when confronted with our mistakes. It is what you do after your mistakes that make the difference because every mistake you make, should be a learning experience, not something that makes you less capable. It is always how you correct your life mistakes or what you learn from them that in the end defines you.

I am going to talk a bit more here about lying to yourself because this is a hard thing to face or even understand because often, we do it, without being conscious, we are doing it. To arrive at a place where you know how to make conscious choices, you must first understand, it is your unconscious choices that have led you to where you are now. We have established this place is separate from you and is somewhere lost in your mind. Self-deception is a personality trait that involves many unconscious motivational false beliefs, mixed in with a contradictory conscious belief. You know deep down that you are lying to yourself. You are an expert at disguising this. It is so much easier than rocking the internal boat you are permanently stuck on, in those choppy waters of your mind. But the boat is rocking so much now, you feel a little sick and want to jump off. You fear you have no safety net to catch you and bring you safely to shore, so the unconscious lying becomes the unconscious objector. The niggling voice inside your head that knows how to make you feel uncomfortable and permanently anxious.

We lie to ourselves to prevent us having to face our mess, rather than owning up or growing up and often it is automatic without conscious thought. If we do find the courage to be honest with ourselves, telling the truth might change everything and maybe not in our favour. We might suddenly fear what we might lose, materially, if we come clean. We are all guilty of telling little white lies now and again, often to get what we desire in the moment. We tell a trivial lie to prevent hurting someone's feelings but lying to ourselves is very different. While most of us can distinguish fact and lie, the self-deceiver needs to make sure that the fact can be hidden, and the lie can be supported. Often, we convince ourselves that the deception, the lie, is true and we have no need to maintain the truth, so we relax and focus on other things. These lies must go somewhere, so in the end, they end up in the unconscious and often leads to telling more lies, to cover up the first lie.

When situations become more stressful, we tend to lie to ourselves even more. Our conscious memory always involves subjective awareness in the recollection of any experience, but the unconscious memory involves retrieval, without awareness, which obviously affects our behaviour. Lying or self-deception puts false information in the conscious mind, whereas the truth ends up in the unconscious.

When your motivation for deception is over, the truth comes back into the conscious. It is normal human behaviour to have emotional attachments to many different beliefs, some of which might be irrational, so our self-deception can serve to help us cope, when confronted with strong feelings of shame. At the end of the day, lying to ourselves to get through life, as a self-protection mechanism, eventually becomes a form of self-sabotage and betrayal. It denies our reality. Once we deceive ourselves, we become our own worst enemy, we end up believing is a friend, not a danger to our mental health. Lying can often involve the complete denial of the hard truths we cannot face. It helps to minimize painful memories or projects blame on to others. I told so many lies to myself on my journey out of poverty to the top of the world, many conscious but more unconscious.

I often created illusions in my mind to present to other people about my past, to make me look better than I was, which now makes me cringe. I made up stories and lies to cover the bad behaviour I was not prepared to own. This toxic energy would build inside me, creating feelings of uncomfortable anxiety often too difficult to handle.

I became so good at lying to myself, I often had no idea when I was doing it. That's how good we are at it. I guess I was always fooling myself I was in control, but the truth of the matter was, my inner child was in control, not me. Although she was confident and resilient, good at problem solving, and self-deception to fight to the top, after all she had been acting like an adult from the age of nine, she had little experience in self-reflection. I only had the guts to look back over my life wreckage when I was forced to. It was difficult to recognize, it was all the work of an immature child, not a centred, enlightened, mature adult. This is the reason I have named this chapter the unconscious objector. This is the hidden child inside the onion. The worm inside us all, unconsciously hiding behind layers of an inherited life, causing uncomfortable anxiety we cannot explain. A reservoir of hidden feelings, thoughts, urges and memories that live outside of our conscious awareness influencing every single move me make.

Because of years of creating self-protection mechanisms, building many protective layers, it has caused us to lose sight of who we are as free-thinking adults. We often don't understand what is real from what is an illusion. We have been deceiving ourselves for so long, we have diminished the power to be the directors in our own authentic stories. When we allow our reality to be denied, it always comes back to haunt us in the end. It might be hard right now to imagine you have your younger wounded self, trapped inside your onion, unconsciously pulling your strings, directing your life, without you consciously aware it is happening. Not all of us have a wounded inner child or seriously damaged worm inside, but most of us have never met our younger selves or got to know them. This is because our lives were managed, directed, and constructed by our caregivers or our circumstances. Learning how to face the past without letting it control your present and future, is a challenging step to take but will be the best step you ever take. You finally grow up and stop lying to yourself to get by. You face your mistakes with forgiveness, then turn up in your life with courage, understanding no one is perfect. Looking over your own personal history gives you a clear picture you can always change, no matter what has happened, but it is down to you to do the work.

What do you do when you discover all your fear, past trauma and pain runs deeper than the current events you are experiencing? How do you initiate some healing, when it's your inner child that is screaming out for love, comfort, and acceptance? I know right now you will be feeling uncomfortable and potentially confused to the idea you must reconnect with someone; you thought you left behind years ago. Or someone you have put on a pedestal and created a fake story about for your whole life. It might even be someone who you have no recollection of, cannot remember, have no real memories of or feelings for. But trust me, acknowledging your inner child, your worm, that niggling feeling pulling at your heart strings, and controlling your life, needs acknowledging now with love.

Pushing your issues, whatever they are, from the past, further under the layers, will only work for so long before they begin to cause you all kinds of emotional problems. If you have suffered abuse, neglect, or any kind of trauma, big or small as a child or your life has been built on the hopes and dreams of others, it is now necessary to be realistic about why and what really happened back then. Travelling down memory lane is not going to be easy and you may be too depressed or anxious to even think about it, but you must be brave during this process recognising, even those from perfect backgrounds will discover many wounds and scares.

We must allow ourselves to revisit that vast void inside and fully acknowledge it for what it is. You may need a therapist to help you with this Journey. It will manifest many unexpected feelings and emotions to the surface from anger, resentment, loss, shame, fear, emptiness, embarrassment, or sadness. If you cannot afford or find the right therapist for you, it is possible to start your inner work alone in private, just make sure you are ready. I am going to use a case study at the end of this journey of my own personal experience, finding my mature authentic self. This might help you to see just how incredible the experience can be and will encourage you to think about trying it for yourself to find peace.

How would you like your life to look in one year from now? How would you like it to be different? If you never consciously define and then create the things you want to change, your unconscious objector, the worm, the inner child beliefs, will continue to create them for you. The sooner you clearly define your dream destination in life, the clearer the intent, the quicker your progress will be. By dream life, I am talking more about a life less focused on what you want materially but more focused on what you need emotionally to grow wiser and mature beyond your past.

We have all, at some point, experienced self-doubt and been left feeling uncertain about ourselves and where we fit in this world. We have all questioned our capabilities and potential, believing we cannot change what is already set in stone. Every time we make major mistakes in life, we lose more confidence in our ability to succeed and eventually we stop trusting in ourselves because we feel inadequate. This vicious cycle of self-doubt ends up being that unbearable, unkind voice in your head, which ends up making you lose all faith in yourself. That vicious voice is NOT you. Every time you try to get something right and you fail because you react over responding, then you feel even more of a failure, just remember, this is not your fault so own it. By looking over your mistakes without feeling like a total failure, you get to see it is a pattern, probably connected to something you learned as a response in childhood.

You have now been on a journey with me to the center of your world. The place where it all began. Along this journey you have been given tools to help you reconnect with your mind, your emotions, and your feelings, through self-reflection, meditation, breathing and personal development. All this sounds so simple, but I know it is not. I know how long it can take to recover from discovering potentially your whole life to date, is not the life you truly desire or even like.

I worked with addicts who are so lost, it would take a bomb going off to just wake them up. I have seen how past pain can cripple minds and ruin lives, but I have also seen incredible results from self-determination and mind transformations.

Once you begin to experience your own life through the lens of acceptance, you are freed from the mental prison of unworthiness. I could get spiritual here and spout many incredible reasons to connect with your higher self, but you are not there yet; that pleasure is to come in my next book. It is a win-win situation when you start to work on yourself because you finally get to feel some power inside and that's something you may have never felt before. You have always had the power inside to do anything you desire; you just need to feel it for yourself to help push you forward beyond your mind.

Poor mental health leaves us afflicted by debilitating feelings of insignificance, inadequacy, and hopelessness. When we are struggling and suffering from a mental disorder, the psyche, the mind, and body, are trying hard to work through the issues and help us to find out the nature of the cause. We have already established that the cure for our mental health issues consists of rectifying the imbalance of psyche energy, helping the ego to integrate with the unconscious mind's contents. Understanding the cause, is an individual process because we all have different issues, on different levels but by reconnecting with your inner child, you can begin to understand yourself better. Once you can see yourself as two separate people, one younger, damaged, and unconscious, one older, damaged, and unconsciously malfunctioning because of the younger one, you can easily begin to recognize your issues and mistakes are not your fault. It is a complicated process but works in the end because you heal and resolve, not remain lost in the dark without complete control over your own life.

When you are disconnected from yourself, you must recognize that your relationship with yourself needs urgent attention. Do you recognize these feelings? Chronic self-doubt with a harsh inner voice that will never shut up? Negative self-image? A pattern of dysfunction behaviours? A lack of real purpose? Constant anxiety? Bouts of depression? Mood swing? Unexplained anger? Frustration? Sorrow? Regrets? Daydreaming over facing reality? Addicted? Stressed when overwhelmed with emotions?

You may not recognize all these symptoms but by checking the current state of your mental health and getting some clarity from reaching further inside, will be the best thing you ever do for yourself. You will finally see yourself in the light, no longer lost in the darkness of the past.

We all need to find enlightenment through self-realization before we leave this dimension. Getting to know the younger self is a positive start. The concept of enlightenment, basically waking up from that coma you have been in for too long, is synonymous with self-realization, or the recognition of your authentic self. The true essence of just being. A real chance to finally see through the false self, the many layers of social conditioning and inherited beliefs, which have tainted your true being for too long. This awaking from your coma will eventually provide you with an intense clarity and a new connection, not only with yourself but with other people too. This is the most amazing part of wiping the slate clean and starting again, you begin to identify with your authentic core values and your own beliefs, not those handed to you at birth. You can decide what is right for you. You can see beyond your anxiety, recognising it is not real but unconsciously arrives because of feeling out of control inside.

We can never be perfect, that is not reality, but we can be better and continue to work hard on developing the things we care about and the people we want to become. There is no joy in being depressed. There is no peace in feeing anxious. There is no point in blaming others. There is no light in the dark. We have all experienced, through life a wide range of emotions, from happiness to fear, anger to addictions with strong dopamine response to keep us going when things get tough.

Self-love is more powerful, more profound, more life changing and way more intense than any fake high. Loving yourself helps you to stabilize your negative behaviours and keeps you away from seeking so much comfort. Learning to truly love yourself comes from truly understanding yourself and we do this by the acceptance, we all have problems. We are all the same. We all have a journey to travel and a story to tell. None of us are perfect. We have all made mistakes, the biggest being we believe we are functioning well, when inside we are living through hell. Very few of us reach out for help and in my own experience, this was a big mistake. I should have reconnected with my inner child so much earlier, to look over my memories, heal, then put them to rest.

I suggest when reconnecting with your younger self, and this will not be easy, you write a long kind forgiving letter to him or her and say goodbye. Letting go of the inner you, buried deep inside, under your unconscious thoughts, feelings, and beliefs, takes enormous courage and forgiveness. You may not be able to manage it straight away. It is going to bring up some pain that might take you back down but remember, you are an adult now.

It is your responsibility to face the past and recognize whatever is causing you pain, is not and I repeat NOT your fault. You are now the healer as an adult who has survived, and it is your job now to grow beyond whatever you endured back then. The past is NOT going to ruin your future, anymore.

If you think back to an earlier chapter, it is the formative years of our childhood up to nine years old, that we learned about our emotions, our safety and who we are. We also learned to make our first connections with others, especially our caregivers and siblings. When an experience during this period feels unsafe and no one helps us through it with comfort, the pain we experience can last for years and eventually create mental health problems in adulthood. This is not always about serious neglect or abuse from caregivers, unsafe experiences can happen to us all in childhood from, losing a parent, divorce, control, addiction issues, sibling rivalry, feeling unloved, no memory of childhood happiness. There are many experiences that can linger unconsciously and then not only eat away at us inside but helps us to create protective layers, as ways to cope. When we write the goodbye letter, after acknowledging the younger self exists, we can offer them the comfort now they may have needed back then. Once you can see what makes you instantly angry or upset, afraid or anxious, you can begin to trace it back to the negative experiences you may have felt, in your childhood. Perhaps your caregiver never gave you praise or hugged you enough, so now you end up feeling rejected, every time someone close to you is too busy to give you attention.

Once you can identify where your pain originated that has created irrational, unbalanced reactions, and emotions you cannot manage, keeping you trapped in pain in adulthood, in the goodbye letter you can tell your inner child, they are safe now and finally heard. It may sound strange to say goodbye to something that is a part of your past but if the unconscious memories are causing you to malfunction, and you cannot control the pain, moving on is the only solution.

We don't choose to be depressed. We don't choose to feel anxious. We don't choose to harm ourselves. We don't choose to live with internal pain. It all must originate somewhere along the journey of life. By travelling back, peeling off layers, consciously thinking, being completely honest, your coping mechanisms along the way will have now changed, as you finally reconnect with your authentic self. You no longer need to hang on to anxiety or depression for comfort because it no longer comforts you. You have understood clearly why you are hurt. You have recognized it is not helping you reach your true potential. You have also learned it is not your fault. You are free to be who you were always meant to be and that is a great stress relief. Depression is something we all suffer from to some degree, usually because we have regrets, feel unfulfilled, don't get what we want but life is too short to live it in the darkness. We must learn to look inward more not outward for answers and talk openly to others about how we are feeling.

One of the main reasons depressions is so debilitating is because the core symptoms make it so hard to ask for help to find a way out. When combination of lethargy, sadness, emptiness, and intense feelings of hopelessness take over, it can challenge the most determined, strongest human spirit. The social isolation that occurs because of depression, just feeds it even more, making recovery even harder. Never feel alone, regardless of how alone you believe you are. You have the power inside to be an independent thinker, just like the day you were born.

Life and circumstances may have got in the way and clouded your view of yourself but underneath all this accumulated rubble, is where you find hope. If you never let go of the past or make peace with it, it will haunt you in depression for the rest of your days. All that negative energy will eventually weigh you down. It will stop you and hinder you from leading a life of fulfilment, achievement, and purpose.

If you have concluded after reading this book that your life still has no meaning, you may be struggling with a lack of purpose. This lack of purpose will eventually affect all aspects of your life and can cause you to ruminate on your anxious thoughts, causing you more distress and pain. We all need a purpose to be here. It is vital to our mental health and well-being because it creates a more fulfilled way to live our lives. I want you to remember now about your core being, your powerful energy source. Life and substance are ideas of the unscrambled mind. Life is about the parts we play, and substance is the thing to be acted upon. Your life is now more about positive clean energies, that propel you towards all your actions, rather than the lethargy your burdens create, keeping you stuck with your pain for comfort. You are not a robot without a heart or a pulse. You are not insignificant in this world, no matter what you think. There is so much more to you, you just don't know it yet. Your true job on this journey of life is to travel beyond your inherited beliefs, to finally discover what underpins everything you think and do.

Look with curiosity at what is often outside your objective experiences and beyond the perception of your reality. Learn to slow down, take a breath, and relax, things can only get better, if you do the work required. Purpose comes with peace of mind. It is an essential part of a fulfilling life. Your life purpose consists of the central motivating aims of your life. Basically, the reason you wake up every day. It is a powerful guide to help with all your life decisions and will influence your behaviour and shape your future goals. It will offer you a sense of direction which then creates more meaning in your life. It's a concept you create to get beyond the mundane day to day trials and tribulations of this thing called life.

Take time in your meditation to explore the nooks and crannies inside your mind and why you put up with your trials and tribulations. Your life must be about more than just being content with things you don't like but believe cannot be changed. Start to empower yourself with the tools and techniques you have been given on this journey, to enhance your awareness, change your perceptions, increase your personal performance, and most importantly, improve your well-being.

From a purely logical place, the fundamental meaning of your life is experience. The concept of experience is related to the concepts of awareness, focus and attention. Being alive and experiencing is the basic minimum to fulfil our adequate achievements. It is the basic purpose of the meaning of life but to truly find authentic happiness, hope, and peace, we must always think about going beyond the minimum, otherwise we end up back in the doldrums. We must ask more profound questions about our existence. To explore more behind the meaning of life, we must recognize our materialistic perspective has taken us away from our purpose and left us empty, depressed, in debt personally and as a world. We cannot honestly eliminate the possibility of the unknown, beyond what we perceive is reality. There must be more to life, surly?

Even though there is no scientific evidence that there is life after death or more to us and the universe, I experienced a near death event that changed me forever. This gave me hope. If we are made up of energy, then I saw this energy leave my own body for a short time, during my near-death event. I therefore believe, based on this event, the meaning of my life is defined by the degree to which I can express the positive curious side of my nature. Always promoting the health and well-being of my powerful, precious energy. I now use a combination of logic, science, and metaphysis to understand the nature of my future reality, not just believing I am a one dimensional know it all. I am open, free, and ready to face whatever life throws at me. I don't chase dreams anymore; I make my dreams come true.

As curious human beings, there may come a time when we begin to question our purpose for being here in the world and what existing truly means. This can come to light when an existential crisis happens, or we begin to lose direction because we cannot figure out the meaning to it all.

This can leave us with utterly pointless thoughts and feelings, we cannot control or satisfy. This is then why we feel depressed, hopeless, or just fed up with our lives. I am hoping if these feelings or thoughts have crossed your mind, this book has helped prevent such thoughts by making you understand you are part of something so much bigger than yourself. I cannot give you all the answers to the meaning of life but at least you can now explore the idea, there can be so much more to life than what you do every day and what you perceive is real from the wreckage of your reality.

We will always perform poorly in life if we live under stress. Anxiety is the underlying feeling which help creates the mistakes we make. It is now time for you to see the errors of the past, as wisdom for the future. Remember, your brain is set to assume that the mistakes you have previously made in the past are the correct way to perform a task, causing an automatic mistake pathway. You are what you think, so it is vital you change your habitual thinking habits so you can approach things in a new way.

Today, I believe failure is a precursor of success. One of life's great ironies. In life you sometimes succeed and sometimes you fail, that is just life. If we can learn from our failures, find the courage to laugh and then the determination to get back up to try again, eventually success will arrive. It is only when our failures become a forgone conclusion that we remain unable to succeed and that is just common sense. As much as you may believe your goals seem too far to reach, remember failure can distort your perception of what you believe you can achieve. Once you fail, you are likely to access your skills and capability incorrectly, so always ask yourself questions. Why did I fail? What made me fail? Is it my perception of my ability? By asking yourself questions like these, you no longer listen to the unconscious objector, stuck in your mind, you begin to recognize your power. Our behaviour is driven in part by thoughts and feelings, which provide insight into our individual psyche, our unique energy, which reveals our true attitude and values.

The truth is personal maturity beyond the wounded child inside is all about, embracing and understanding, your core values that align with your personal growth, are as important as eating healthy and psychical exercise. The exploration of knowledge brings wisdom, essential for all who wish to achieve a life worth living rather than a life of stagnant beliefs and behaviours. Before my own life-changing event, I was desperately attempting to create a life of contentment and happiness. At the beginning of the maturing process, much of my past could not be fixed directly through just meditation. Instead, I found that most of my authentic self was hidden and wrapped deeply beneath the many layers of my onion. The fragmented dimensions and realities that I had learned to exist with. At first this was disturbing. I was constantly on edge because I could see I was trapped in a cycle that was unverifiable to my conscious mind. It took me ages to clear my mind and quieten down the unconscious objector, so don't give up if you find the meditation process is not working. You will get there and when you do, you too will see more clearly the things that have been causing you inner turmoil and unexplained anxiety. Just remember, the greatest moments in your life will be found on the edge of fear.

I truly urge you to take the time to explore your mind, your mistakes, your thoughts, your actions, and your inability to control your emotions. Learn to exercise your capability to explore the universe and why you are here because once your physical body becomes useless, you will be stuck with only your mixed-up mind. It is time you reclaim your life and work towards being a free thinker. When we are born, the world seems just as it should be because our every need is met by our caregivers. As we grow up into adults, what this world is and what the world should be, begins to change but often we don't change with it. A big part of the growing up process, is to eliminate fears and bring our impulsive desires under control because fear cultivates ignorance and desire gets you into trouble. Real freedom involves control over your whole life, learning to make decisions and then take personal responsibility for your actions, the consequences. We will never be remembered, go down in history, unless we are committed to a life full of meaningful things. You cannot have a meaningful life, without a way to make your own meaningful imprint in the sand.

I know you will find the right meaningful path to inner peace through your own self-discovery journey. It won't be easy but hopefully now you can at least begin to think more openly and more deeply, as to why you are here and what you need to do to be free from your inherited beliefs. Life has no meaning, each of us has meaning and we bring it to life.

"It is a waste to be asking the question when YOU are the answer." - Joseph Campbell.

CHAPTER NINE

Everything happens for a reason, or does it?

Our actions today are determined by what has been programmed into us from birth. Failure is ego threatening, which will cause us to zone out. Lying to ourselves is an unconscious psychological defence mechanism that protects us against painful or intolerable feelings. Self-deception always evolves to enable us to persuade others, if we start believing our own lies, it is much easier to get others to believe them, too.

Shame can lead us to hide our mistakes from others, which can be a highly destructive combination. Once you are hiding your mistakes, you not only never learn from them, but often you make them worse, either through attempts to cover them up or through a misguided effort to correct them. Learn to separate your self-worth from your mistakes.

Once you have done everything you can, to right your mistake and learn as much as possible about how to never do it again, you can move on confidently with a clear conscience. Learn to be authentic. How we balance authenticity and our mental well-being throughout our lives and across the many roles we play, will always bring huge life challenges. We must learn to embrace the reality of our dysfunctional anxieties, inherited beliefs, and lack of maturity to become fully responsible for how we choose to live.

You are the product of who everyone else has told you to be. All these messages are internalized and become your own inner critic, telling you how you should think, act, and behave. The outcome of this noisy negative chatter in your mind of self-judgement and untruths in the end, undermines your self-esteem. It is a conflict between your powerful unconscious memories and your authentic conscious power, constantly wearing you down and becoming uncontrollable anxiety: the worm inside your onion.

Know yourself, what you are good at, what you are prepared to do, and what you are not prepared to do. Learn to face up to the truth of who you are, without self-judgement. Honesty is not always easy to face or pleasant, but it has the potential to set you free. Everything happens for a reason in this thing called life.

Or does it?

Self-analysis is not something that everyone can face, by now you might be feeling either lighter yourself or even more confused but whatever you are feeling, at least you are feeling something. When you are motivated towards creating more fulfilment in your life and you learn to self-actualize, you recognise it is a normal experience, yet it can remain unrecognised when our needs are not satisfied.

We live in this mad, materialistic world where life is often hard to navigate; we end up giving up the fight to be heard, to be free, to be mindful and happy. How we perceive our reality, our authenticity, is a vital part of who we are because not only does it influence what pleasure we gain from our experiences, it also predetermines our judgments and behaviour. We will do almost anything to survive, to get through our lives, often without ever authentically taking part in it and this is a truly scary concept.

We have gone through the layers created by others, our circumstances, our inherited beliefs, and our mind's madness to arrive at a place we can begin to understand ourselves better.

We have hopefully understood that love from our caregivers, the people we trusted without any hesitation, is often conditional and, by this, I mean we are often shown love when we perform well or please others.

This then means that we learn to do things to feel a sense of belonging and acceptance, rather than using our own instincts to make decisions that are right for us authentically. We often end up putting on a show to please others and when we do find the courage to speak out, be ourselves, we often get into conflict because we go against the grain. We find it hard to be an independent thinker, have our own opinions, beliefs, and ideas of who we are. This creates feelings of isolation, and the ego pops up to help you cope. I have been trying throughout this journey to help you understand the importance of getting to know the real you, under all this pretence, life conditioning and unnecessary baggage.

If others don't get you, then that is their issue and not yours. I do understand we all need to feel accepted, understood, admired, and included but if you must change who you are for this to happen, all you are doing is lying to yourself. We have already gone over what this does to your self-esteem, so let us just remember here, we are as good as anybody else and deserve to be heard without judgment. Never manipulate your life to fit in and be authentic, show up as yourself and stand your ground until others come to you.

They will, trust me.

I hope by now you understand the things that are necessary in your own life to nurture happiness and personal success. I hope you are beginning to get to know yourself, so you can be yourself, like yourself more and believe in yourself, confidently owning everything that is real about you. Living an unauthentic life is so damaging to your mental well-being, in fact, it is more damaging than you could ever imagine. I truly know for a fact that other people, when you show up as yourself, vulnerable and honest, admire and are drawn to your powerful energy, so don't be fearful of change.

Things always happen for a reason, another lovely cliché. I love this one because it is true when you are living life for real and not just blindly going through the motions to please others. Now that worm is out of your onion and you have examined, uncovered, healed, and let go of the past, you are free to make your own choices without fear of being told off or made to feel a failure.

You are NOT a failure, you are someone who can express their own views, opinions as the confident being you are. Once you can show vulnerability and humility without fear, you are hard-wired to make much stronger human connections with those who you attract into your life. Those who still try and dehumanize you or put you down will come round in the end; just be brave enough to stand alone and continue to be a better person.

I hope you are beginning to feel braver now because standing alone, vulnerable, not really knowing what you are doing, asleep for most of your life, is tough. Keep focused until you change your mind.

As humans, we depend on others for our survival, but this has many downsides. Always remember fear comes from abandonment issues in childhood. You need people obviously, we all do, but not as much as you might think. Attracting the right people into your life can be a game changer because they will be likeminded and allow you to be yourself, the real key to happiness.

Anxiety, the worm, is the biggest component of fear, characterized by insecure, distorted thinking patterns. We have learned that these distorted thinking patterns create irrational presumptions not only about ourselves but about other people.

Being alone is a good thing, especially during your self-analysis journey. You will have difficulty controlling your emotions and feel a little unstable at times but remember, keep yourself above the issues and become the silent observer looking down.

It is important to go over the groundwork we have done in the book before we end, so you can continue to work on the new you in private. What you have learned throughout this journey will help you to identify your thinking patterns and distortions, so you can begin to replace them with more adaptive thinking patterns. This is so effective for treating anxieties, depression and improving your ability to change perspectives, thus improving your internal communication patterns.

Self-awareness is your only goal now. You are going to be completely involved in your own life, how you think, how you make choices, how you respond, never react and how you wish to be seen by others. Remember, you are NOT a preconditioned robot with no control over your life. You are not lost at sea without a life jacket; you are present, solid and in control of every single thought you have, every behaviour and every action. You are now part of something much bigger than just little old lost you.

I want you to think about your old brain like a dead plant in the garden of your life. It was once a beautiful, simple part of nature that would blossom without you doing anything. It just needed sunlight, love, and energy to survive. This old brain is of no use to you now. It is not healthy or alive but riddled with worms who have eaten every bit of what was once incredible. It is time to put this dead plant back into some new healthy soil, somewhere you can see it every day and watch it slowly come back to life. As the new green shoots of life begin to emerge into the sunlight, you can keep reminding yourself that you are emerging into the world beyond the past, beyond the pain, and begin to visualize the life you deserve. This visualization technique will help provide insight to the irrational thoughts you once had that led you to mistrust not only yourself but others too. It will help you to develop a better understanding of the thoughts you had and the behaviours of others because of these thoughts.

You are no longer dictated to by the mess, the past, the anxiety, the depression, the lack of meaning, you have a new brain to develop, new knowledge, a new understanding of yourself, the real you, the authentic you. It will be scary as I have already said but not as scary as dying without ever meeting yourself.

We have established that meaning in life is a concept that you create for yourself. It is about having a purpose for being here. It is about not being dragged under the carpet of depression because everything feels hopeless and impossible. I am sure all your doubts about the meaning of your life are underpinned with many of the things we have learned together. I am also sure you have never really challenged your mind. When you really think about this, it is quite astounding, but it is often the case.

Carl Jung did his very best to encourage us all to become independent thinkers. To become whole. To be conscious of the unconscious. He helped put me back together and today I am so alive I can hardly stand it at times. I never feel those surges of emotion anymore. I never look outward for someone else to make me happy. I keep myself to myself but still enjoy other people, always being conscious to be myself and never judge or blame. It has taken me a long time and has not been an easy transition, but today I understand wholeheartedly that facing and forgiving all my life mistakes is what real transformation looks like.

Forgiving myself and others truly did change me. I was small minded. Even though I was a go-getter, ambitious, successful, and accomplished, I often habitually blamed others for my own misfortunes. In the bigger scheme of things, I was an average thinker until I learned to dedicate myself to a life filled with wisdom, understanding that my impulse to blame others for my mistakes, meant there was nothing to be gained. I knew I couldn't travel backwards in time to fix my mistakes, but I found peace and enlightenment in the knowledge I had learned from them and by doing so, I got to really know myself. It is never a weakness to forgive yourself. It is a testament to just how strong you really are.

As you know by now, I am a student at the school of life and will continue to attend until my energy leaves this dimension called life.

If you had the opportunity right now to be looking down on your dead body from above, just as I was privileged to do, what regrets would you have? Would you feel gratitude and satisfaction or regret and remorse? How much of your life would you have wasted not really participating or driving your own destiny bus? Would you want to return and restore your ability to develop inner calm, clear insight, and all judgement from your suffering? These are all questions you should be asking yourself right now, not when you are dead. It is too late then. Self-dialogue, contemplation of such things as your death, the only thing you can rely on to certainly happen one day, is a kind of meditation aimed at disciplining your mind to remain in the present. The here and now.

We have arrived at this place, through this journey, to learn how to free ourselves from unhealthy desires. We have learned that we must accept then be flexible with the path of our lives without losing track of who we are. We must surrender ourselves to the full flow of the powerful energies we produce and happily liberate ourselves of the ego, to find answers to our pessimistic, inherited beliefs, finally feeling happiness for real. The truth is most of us have been suffering much more in our imagination than in our reality. This is so true when you begin to believe authentically above what you desire.

I have understood and I hope by now you may be thinking in the same direction, all our suffering is caused by our attachment to our life situations, family, friends work, desires and all these things then create nothing but more anxiety and worry. Sadly, the biggest source of our suffering comes from ignorance of our innate power and courage to stand alone and shine beyond all doubt and fear.

Don't waste any more time. Don't let the sand of time slip through your fingers. Life is not short, we have plenty of time, we just waste so much of it trying to be something we are not. Life is so exciting, once you can recognise and accept that one day you will leave. But always remember, your energy never dies, only your flesh, blood, and bones.

Stop saying you are fine when asked how you are by others, Start talking about how you feel. Be open to change and never envy what you see in others. Instead, love what you see in yourself. Don't postpone things you say you want to experience. Delete your imaginary illusions and desires then replace them with action driven possibilities. Plant them in the new brain you are growing in the garden of your life. Make time for more wisdom in your life. You have allowed so much unnecessary anxiety, regret, depression, and misery to dictate your personality for too long. I hope now you are more aware of the concept of time and will be able to freely focus on that which is timeless and limitless. I hope you can begin to recognise you are eternal and go far beyond time.

Before I tell you about my own thought-provoking journey in the final chapter of this book, I must say this: although in some ways I believe things happen for a reason, my more spiritual self is beginning to question this, as I grow and explore new ideas.

Our brains are already wired, as we have already established, to look for reasons but many things do happen through random chance or what we know as, good, or bad luck.

Is everything pre-determined? When I looked back over my own car crash life, many of the events were determined by the choices I made but my brain was wired a certain way because of things that had happened to me in the past. It is true that the way in which we have remembered the past does limit our free will.

We have free will to make better choices, so we must learn to make better choices. Only then will things happen for the right reasons because we have consciously done the right thing. I can conclude both options are true. We unconsciously choose negative experiences and then realize after we have dealt with the consequences that we have learned important lessons. This then tells us; everything happens for a reason. You picked up this book for a reason. Maybe you liked the cover. Maybe you liked the title. Maybe you were at a crossroads. Or maybe you just like reading books. Whatever the reason, there was one. I hope the reason has produced freer will in the future choices you make in your life.

All our behaviour has a cause and effect. Our free will and what we choose to do and say will always determine the outcome. Overall, all that happens to us have reasons for their existence.

I came out of my own life-changing experience a much better person because I was forced to learn the true meaning of self-destruction and heartbreak. I was comforted with learning how to forgive myself, something I believed I'd never be able to do. I was drowning in my own mistakes, lost in my own doubt and under pressure to feel better. I learned nothing is forever. I had a brutal lesson in loss, which made me better, but I never looked in the mirror until recently and said, "Everything happens for a reason."

Yes, everything happens for a reason, but we still have free will. I am a free spirit today with the ability to make the right choices for me but if I ever veer too far off the path of my personal journey to enlightenment, the universe, the bigger picture, always guides me back. So, what is the bigger picture to you? Hopefully after reading this book, it describes the widening of your perspective to get you closer to a clearer view of what really matters and what doesn't in your mind.

It allows you to consider as many perspectives as possible to learn to develop a deeper understanding of all sides of the truth. Looking at the bigger picture absolutely increases your self-awareness and as we have established, gives you better control over your feelings, behaviour and, ultimately, your actions. With increased self-awareness, you begin to encounter a calmness inside which dilutes your often unexplained anxiety.

I learned to look at every situation I encountered as a whole picture and not just the bits I wanted to see. This happened because studies have shown that stronger feelings of having meaning in life leads to both significantly higher mental and physical health. I had experienced this for myself.

I also learned, looking at the bigger picture, that it is so easy to get wrapped up in arguing with others over minor disputes or opposing opinions. But it is much healthier and more beneficial to find a common ground which strengthens relationships, rather than destroying them. Asking yourself questions during self-analyses is critical when looking at your own problems in the bigger picture.

Ask yourself daily what problems you are encountering. What is the real root cause of these problems? Are you sure the problems you face are right? Is there a solution you might be missing to solve the problem? Is your perspective of the problem real? Are you thinking big enough or are you being small minded yourself? Is your perspective of your problem overshadowed by your ego?

Remember, your new brain in your garden of life is to be kept tidy, focused, in tune with your feelings, positive and never allowed to be strangled by random weeds of self-doubt. You are teaching your subconscious mind new pathways, new words, new feelings: all of which will eventually become the new you. Start telling yourself that you love your life. You love your problems. You love your depression. You love your job. You love your body. Your love your mind. Do this even if you don't believe it. And keep doing it.

By doing this continually and religiously, you begin to change the way you speak to yourself. This will create positive good feelings inside which will tell your subconscious mind you are happy and then give you back the feelings that go with feeling happiness. If you keep saying that you hate your life, your subconscious mind will hear you, believe you and keep you feeling like you hate your life. We are what we think, remember. What you put in, you get back, its simple.

Finally, your conscious mind is everything you are aware of in the world around you and everything you think right now.

For example, you might be consciously aware that you shouldn't be drinking a bottle of wine, but you do it anyway. You only use ten percent of your conscious brain at any one time, and this is why it has been so hard for you to get on top of your thinking, emotions, and negative behaviours. The subconscious part of your mind is a huge storage bank, like your computer. It stores information that you are not currently thinking about but can flow into your conscious awareness at any time.

You may, for instance, have decided consciously to only have one glass of wine, but you are subconsciously aware when you have had three or four and shouldn't have. Your unconscious mind is the problem and what we have been trying to see more of on this journey together. It is made up of automatic processes that the conscious mind cannot access because they happen underneath your conscious awareness: the place where the worms live, your suppressed thoughts, feelings and emotions that control automatic everyday behaviours without us being consciously aware it is happening.

For example, you consciously decide to have one glass of wine but subconsciously go on to have three, even though you know you are aware of the decision you made to only have one. The problem arrives when you have lost control because you want to forget and unconsciously drank the whole bottle plus one more and find yourself unconscious.

It is important to understand how your mind works on this self-analysis journey because then you can begin to understand why you are struggling to take back control of your life to find more meaning and authentic happiness. So, once again, like Carl Jung said: until we make the unconscious, conscious it will direct your life and you will call it fate.

CHAPTER TEN

A thought-provoking journey

Finding the sunshine in the dark clouds of a storm, is no different to finding a needle in a haystack. I am not a qualified psychologist, but I have had the great privilege to work with people who put their trust in me because I cared enough about them and their happiness to want to do the work. I am passionate about the world of business, but my purpose is to help those struggling with the meaning of life. The more work I do with people who are functioning but not realizing their full potential, the more I recognize how important self-analysis is.

Looking after, and maintaining work on your car or your home, we all take very seriously and are then proud of what we do. I am interested in finding out more about why human beings have not worked as hard to take care of their mental health, which in many cases, is the reason for physical poor health.

We are extremely lucky in the western world, in terms of being provided everything we need to survive, unlike the poor and starving around the rest of the world who don't even have clean water to drink. So, why is it that although we have everything we need, huge opportunities to basically do whatever we want, we choose to be more preoccupied with other people's lives, seemingly wanting what they have, more. I do understand myself, why money will never buy what we need to be happy. I experienced the ugly world of capitalism myself and it became partly responsible for my extraordinary downfall.

Growing up as a child of the fifties, money was not the most important factor in life. Yes, we had to have money to survive but never more than we needed. Going to work, working hard, and having a good time as a family, was much more of a priority than constantly stressing about what others we perceived had, more than we had. Life was so much simpler than it is today, and I am truly grateful to have experienced both poverty and, unimaginable wealth in my lifetime to date. You might be thinking here money would solve all your problems and I am mad to say the opposite but trust me, money is great but truly understanding yourself, is greater.

I wanted to end this book looking more into my own life and my mistakes, as a case study, to try and explain what the meaning of life is to me, after experiencing both sides of the coin.

Let's go back and look at how different life was in the fifties when I was born, to how it is today. Although I have very little recollection of my feelings back then, I do have some powerful memories, that carved out the long and winding road to the top of the world. Family life was very different back then, especially for my poor mother who did all the washing for six children and two adults by hand, instead of the convenience of using a washing machine. Can you imagine? We didn't have a fridge, so food was bought by her daily from the butcher, baker, and candlestick maker. Sugar rationing after the war had only just finished and there was no spare money for treats, trips, or toys. If you wanted to find out what was going on in the world outside of the street you lived on, you only had the radio or a newspaper for ideas, both expensive and seen as a luxury. My dad worked his fingers to the bone to provide what we needed to survive life. He never complained. He just went to work at the same time every day and returned home, the same, as he left.

Occasionally as a huge treat, on a Friday, at the end of the work week, we would have fish and chips and eat them out of the paper. There was no such thing as what you fancied, when you fancied, delivered on an app, whilst watching TV, day, or night. Fast food was not even thought about back then, you got what you were given and that was that, like it or lump it.

One main meal a day was all we could afford, after porridge to start the day to getting you going, then stews and broths made from boiled bones, barley and whatever you could grow green, in the back garden.

I do recall, the weather back then was much more consistent than it is today. It was warm in the summer and cold in the winter, no real extreme events but always plenty of rainy dull Sunday afternoons, playing cards and board games to pass the time. My mother, during the cold winters, would hand wash my nappies and then put them out on the line in the back garden to dry, often brought back in frozen solid to thaw in front of a fire she made herself, every day. The chimney sweep would come twice a year with his array of equipment, to unclog the accumulated soot, making it safe to lite, once again.

I do remember fondly back then, the clock ticking, water boiling on the stove, dogs barking, cats howling and children excitedly playing hopscotch in the road. It was life. All we knew, and everyone helped each other out.

Life was constricted in many ways back then. I remember going to see the doctor was seen as a weakness, so the only time

I was ever taken was for inoculations against potential diseases, just like you are taking your pet to the vet today. If you had a cold, you carried on regardless. There was no room at the inn to lounge in bed all day, being pampered and provided potions to comfort you back to health. My mother never indulged our whims or inundated us with stuff to keep us quiet or spoil us. She taught us to be grateful for what we had and taught us to mend anything that was broken, providing good problem-solving skills, later in life.

Life was tough at the beginning of the fifties, after all, we must remember the UK had been bombed to a pulp after the war and was financially broke and morally exhausted. There was no such luxury as going to the bank to borrow money, rationing was just ending and decent housing almost non-existent. Towards the end of the fifties, life was improving as the economy began to build and then to boom. More families had the need for security, after years of enduring war. There was a big shift in more people getting married, having babies, and a housing boom began to emerge. Life was coming back to life, as the money began to flow into the pockets of those who remained focused and worked hard.

I was taught by my mother one important thing: I was special. She always fed me when I was hungry, put me to bed when I was tired and disciplined with words, never corporal punishment. I grew up an independent thinker. I now believe this was down to her simple but never overpowering opinions about what was right for me or what I should be thinking. I had a working-class upbringing, watching both my parents doing the best they could, often under extreme circumstances, most today would struggle to survive, without medicating or complaining.

As I reached around four, we began to see the beginning of the introduction of aspiration, as several mod cons were introduced into the equation, which made life easier for housewives and mothers, completing their daily chores.

It was time to step away from decades of drudgery and jump into a more modern era of fun, with many new possibilities to look forward to. Everything slowly began to change for me. My environment was upgraded from a two bedroomed very small, terraced house in Howard Road, to a brand new four bedroomed council house, on a newly built estate. It was the swinging sixties and my life truly changed overnight, as the people around me began to party, have fun, drink more, smoke more and be merry. The pub became a place to spend relaxing times and I often witnessed my parents drinking just a little too much, which began creating cracks in the idea of their happy-ever-after.

We finally had spare money to go on holidays to the seaside, eight crammed in a caravan. We even got our first television. This was so exciting for me, as it opened my eyes to a whole new world of possibilities, beyond the estate, allowing me to escape from the building tension, between my parents. I began to see, there was so much more to life going on in the outside world. As I began to imagine, a better life beyond, what I already had.

School was always difficult for me and boring. I struggled to fit in. I discovered more later in life, as I began to realize I was dyslexic. So, the television became my only escape from the building misery inside of feeling different.

I emersed myself into the flourishing world of art, music, and fashion, following and emulating colourful emerging designers and models like Mary Quant, Jean Shrimpton, and Twiggy. I had four older siblings who played loud music on the small record player day and night, from the Beatles to Elvis. My mother loved to sing, dance and party with the neighbours, filling the house with drunken mayhem, often to the disgust of my straitlaced father, who preferred peace and quiet. It was both a tough and exciting time for me but nothing damaging occurred to disturb my mental health and for that, I am truly grateful.

In the early part of the sixties when I was around eight years old, full of excitement about my future, my mother suddenly left me and my younger sister and took up with our milkman. A happy, cheerful chappie she had been having a secret affair with, behind my father's back, for years. It was a big shock that shook the very foundations of my whole world, leaving my devastated father to pick up the pieces, bringing the two of us up alone. The older siblings had already found new lives and left home for different reasons, siding more with my mother and her milkman than my poor father.

It was suddenly a time of peace, love and rock & roll, after years of the grim realities of war, so I could almost see why it happened, even so young. My mother had left a world of poverty in Glasgow herself at sixteen, to find a better life before marring my father for security and not necessarily, love. She had endured so much internal misery, keeping it all together, supressing her curious, enigmatic personality, in favour of being a cook, slave and bottle washer. I almost secretly admired her for escaping. After all, she had given her best, tried so hard to please everyone else, it was now time for her to have some fun and see something new herself.

The painful realization for my father and younger sister was much more devastating, as both struggled to cope but I just sailed through it all and it was probably here, I created my first mask, persona, layer of pretence. I took on the role as substitute mother to my younger sister, as we didn't see ours for over two years during which time, she suffered a nervous breakdown and was sectioned in a mental hospital. The guilt, shame and menopause all consuming, left her, drained, depressed and devastated, once the realization of her actions hit her, like a bolt of lightning. I wasn't very good at playing mother, but we had my older sister who was on hand when things got too tough to handle. School became increasing tough for me, as I battled my way through my dyslexia issues, creating my next mask, becoming an entrepreneurial teenager.

I have since discovered, many successful entrepreneurs suffer with dyslexia, and now I know why they became so rich without a formal education. You find yourself having to go around the outside of things, to prove you are not stupid and tend to be driven beyond your pain. Dyslexia back then was not really diagnosed or even discussed. If you had trouble learning, you were classed as a dunce and cruelly humiliated by those who should have known better. I knew I wasn't a dunce. In fact, I was both emotionally and intellectually bright, with incredible optimism, insight, and curiosity, but it wasn't enough to shield me from the scolding and suffering of life at school. I made the decision, after being physically punished with a ruler and many times forced into detention, I would find other ways to shine and be popular.

I started selling stuff that everyone wanted but couldn't easily get hold of, like cigarettes and chocolate. My father managed a big cash and carry, so there were always boxes of sweets and crisps to help me create my own private tuck shop, undercutting the school and annoying the uptight head, who hated my guts. I soon became the most popular girl in the school overnight. My dyslexia got lost in the mix of entrepreneurship. By the time I was fourteen, I hardly went to school to be honest and with my father working and my responsibility for my younger sister proving painful for me, I focused more on having a good time, always searching for the way out.

I remember watching a documentary on the BBC, with my father one evening, about the City of London and being glued to the set, eyes wide with curiosity. I had never travelled further than Skegness, which was not the most exciting or glamourous place on the planet. Seeing this bustling, vibrant, cosmopolitan capital, with its tall buildings, city gents in pin-striped suits and bowler hats, shiny leather briefcases and clinking champagne glasses, changed my life. I suddenly knew with clarity, without a shadow of doubt, this was where I belonged one day. I just had to find a way to make it happen.

My father tried to bring me back down to earth with a bang, as I told him I was going to be a banker in a pin-striped suit, become rich enough to change our lives and pay him back for all his personal sacrifices, bringing me up. I didn't take any notice of his advice and made it my only focus, until one day, after some unexplainable, irrational mistakes in my late teens, I moved to London to begin a new life in recruitment. I didn't have the money to just move to London myself. My father was not that keen for me to go, so I dated a few men, based on my looks and charm, until I met someone from London in a cocktail bar, who I moved in with quickly. He was fun and very rich. We had a good time for a couple of years and when it all broke up, he gave me some money to set me up and send me on my way.

He knew I was ambitious, so he helped me secure a really good job with a friend of his in a top recruitment firm. He could see I was fiercely independent and wanted more from life than the marriage and kids he desired himself. The new job paid well and the harder I worked, the more I wanted. The more I wanted, the harder I worked.

I obviously never got to wear the pin-striped suit and bowler hats were no longer in fashion, but I did date many men in my dream city attire and began building my new life, a long way from my humble council estate beginnings.

I can honestly say here, I never thought about anything deep or spiritual and my mind, although focused on success, was never filled with regret or shame. I knew even back then, there was potentially more to life than money and success, but I had watched my own mother yearn for more, walking away from her whole life, without ever looking back. I guess subconsciously, I modelled the same behaviour myself because we had been so close in my early days as a baby. I am sure she would talk to me in my pram, on long walks through the park, about her internal misery, encouraging me to always dream big myself.

Already a skilled entrepreneur with good looks, a great figure, a sharp ruthless mind, and the ability to sell snow to Eskimos, it was not long before I was promoted into a management role, which secured me buying my first London flat. I was so driven and so focused on becoming rich, I neglected my family and only returned periodically to buy them or show off my success. It wasn't easy to fit in with the right set in London, who I knew without doubt would catapult me to my wildest dreams, beyond my council house background. So, I began fudging the truth about my roots, creating many whoppers to fit in and impress anybody who would listen, pushing my authentic self, further behind masks to get on in life.

I did begin to feel some guilt every time I saw my family, especially my younger sister, who had now made it herself beyond university into a marriage and on a teaching path. She was traumatised by the loss of our mother, and I had not been the best support for her because I was too busy myself, struggling to become popular and escape it all.

By the time the exciting eighties and nineties arrived, I was on a role, moving up a golden ladder, buying expensive clothes, driving fast cars, travelling the globe, and dating rich men. My career was going from strength to strength. I was making more money than I could ever have dreamed about, and life was good. During this period, my father and older brother both suddenly died, which forced me to go home and reconnect with my mother and my family. I felt like a fish out of water by now and struggled to be real with them. I didn't fit anywhere anymore, and my authentic self was so compromised because of the wild tales that, by now, I had begun to believe myself. I had such pain and anxiety with the loss of my father because if it had not been for him, pushing me out of bed as a teenager and keeping me grounded, who knows what would have happened to me?

I loved and admired him for never really breaking down after losing my mother to another man. He soldered through his internal battle, and I only ever saw him cry once, on my shoulder, the very day after she walked out. I guess here I can assume, I probably switched off my own emotions to contain my pain and never let anyone do to me what my mother had done to him.

Spending time with my mother and the milkman, at his funeral, was not easy. By now, she was drinking away her sorrow, her pain, and her guilt. The dream of happiness was evidently not materialising for her as she had once imagined it would. I always felt so disconnected from her when I went back and watching her drink to cope made things even worse for me. We never talked about the reality of the situation, all of us in the family had created new lives, jobs and we came together now and again, when I could make it. Two funerals in a short space of time forced me back home to face some pain, I then buried it inside to push forward and continue my journey to the top of the world.

I did get married in the mid-eighties for a short while, between jobs, to someone I met in a bar and decided I wanted to have kids with him and settle down.

I think, to be honest, that this was a big internal warning; my life had become a bit fake and a bit to hectic to for me to handle. I was exhausted trying to climb that golden ladder and just wanted a change of scenery. I wanted someone else to take care of me for a change. I also believe that the pressure of my biological clock and the idea that all my friends had husbands and kids, pushed me into feeling a bit left out and too different to fit in. The life template got me for a few seconds and before you could say Jack Robinson, I was a married sheep, following the route to an imaginary fairy-tale, happy-ever-after ending.

After discovering I could not have kids, due to blocked fallopian tubes, I woke up from my coma and moved out, back into the big bad world of pin-striped suits and making money. I was already past the middle of the golden ladder and well on the way to the top of the world before getting married, so I easily fitted straight back in, as though nothing had happened.

It's funny this thing called life. I never really understood where my drive came from, until I stopped climbing that ladder. During my mini retirement from work, pretending to be a good wife with a dog, a husband and a big house in a posh street, miles from the council house estate, I suddenly had too much time on my hands.

I would start to reflect and feel uncomfortable inside, sometimes feeling anxious and worried about how I had somehow managed to get so far ahead without a conscience. I began to have sleepless nights, feel guilty, lose sight of my dream. This would then force me to medicate with either booze or pot, sometimes the odd line of coke to soothe and settle the anxiety inside. I was never addicted but needed some help to keep the dark clouds at bay. I should have seen what was coming long before it arrived but the pull of wealth and the need to be successful took over my instincts desperately trying to warn me to stop and think.

Of course, I didn't listen, and I know why now. I would have probably been so depressed, I would have shot myself, so I just kept ignoring the signs and carried on climbing. I had some fun and some short relationships between working hard, always to just escape and have fun, nothing serious with no desire to be tide down, ever again.

During the mid-nineties, the city was booming and with a friend, I set up my own global headhunting firm in the emerging markets, on a £5000 start up investment. My father would have been astounded and proud, I am sure. My mother by this stage was probably too reliant on booze, to understand my true success or how far I had come.

I didn't go home much because I was too busy again making money and buying property. I began investing in the stock market, buying art, travelling first class too far off fabulous places, slowly losing sight of the past.

As the company grew, I travelled to many places like Russia, New York and even Argentina, sometimes encountering experiences beyond my wildest dreams. I had lots of contacts, was invited to the best parties, was a member of the best private clubs and ate in the most expensive restaurants. As the stock market boomed and my shares bought low, on a tip from a broker, reached dizzy heights, I purchased more property, investing in doing them up for a quick sale and more profit. I loved the power of being in control of my life but my mind, by now, I was probably not in control of. I never stopped to check my mental health or if I was exhausted. When I felt anxiety coming on, I would just book a fight to Barbados and crash out on a sunbed for a week, before spending the rest of the trip, obliviously partying the nights away. I loved having money. It made me feel powerful, invincible, and basically untouchable and that's not good for anybody, regardless of what you might be thinking. People think money buys happiness but never really understand what happiness is and I was as guilty as the next man on this.

By the time the late nineties arrived, in mid-life, burnt out, empty inside, riding a wave so huge, I was potentially about to be ruthlessly sucked under, the blustering wind blew in a blast from the past and changed my destiny overnight.

A good girlfriend and ex-employee from my recruitment days, who had been a massive part of my partying days, before I built my own firm, had moved to LA to find herself and a handsome husband. She was a functioning alcoholic with a risky streak, that made her impulsive; sometimes her ideas got her into big trouble but, by chance, she had somehow found the man and was getting married. I immediately took up the opportunity to travel to LA to see her, meet the husband-to-be and, at the same time, escape my reality to have some fun myself. I had always wanted to go to Hollywood and see the bright lights but never got around to it, so this was perfect and off I went without a care. She set me up with some handsome chap she had met whilst working at a dating agency, the same place she got her husband-to-be from, so I would not be lonely and could make up a foursome whilst there. When I arrived, although my date was handsome, he was crazy, just like my friend and her husband-to-be.

She hadn't changed, was still drinking too much, and was marrying a stranger who was not a big drinker himself. I could suddenly hear alarm bells ringing in my ears but went along with it, anyway. I did try and talk her out of it during a late-night drinking session, but it was too late, she was already gone and mad about the boy. She asked me to be the maid of honour at her wedding, informing me, her husband's good-looking brother, was the best man. How could I refuse? Why did I not try harder to stop her making the biggest mistake of her life? I was supposed to be the sensible one. I recognize here, I wanted a change so badly from my exhausting life in the crazy world of city finance, I saw this as another escape, rather than sorting out my head.

I came back to the UK to count my pennies, check my stocks, and run my empire, agreeing to return to LA for her wedding in a few months' time. She suddenly surprised me out of the blue and came to visit a month before the wedding, with the new husband, to introduce me to his good-looking brother. I offered to have them stay with me in my new house, which had just been renovated and was big enough to give them plenty of space. By now I was riding so high on the stock market, cashing in on my property sales and even further away from my authentic self.

My instincts were dead and buried beneath the huge pile of personal success. I wasn't listening or feeling anything, just carrying on climbing higher, towards the top of the world and potentially beyond. My drinking increased, to help relieve the pressure of client entertaining every night. I hated going to stripe bars with clients, late at night, after long boozy dinners and uncontrollable drug taking, by them. I always remained sober and in control and there was a good reason for this. Once the clients were blotto and behaving badly, I was safe from their advances and could often use the mayhem they caused, to tease and humiliate them the following day. This often made them feel so uncomfortable, they would feel embarrassed, sorry and make sure they made up for it with another big fat deal for me.

I was smoking pot to relax late at night when I returned from work and coke occasionally to get me back up there and start again. It was a yo-yo existence of getting up there, before crashing back down. Never stopping to breath, let alone reflect. The party from LA arrived and it was wild for a couple of days, rushing here and there, showing off my wealth and having fun with my friend before she got married. I could see she was drinking even more than before she left. The husband-to-be was not happy.

It was so evident they had nothing in common, both from very different worlds. She was a Yorkshire lass, and he was a Mexican American with some deep hidden issues of anger I tried to uncover but failed miserably to get to the bottom of.

The brother was unusual. A good looking black haired Mexican American charmer who worked as a security door fitter and relaxed by riding his Harley Davidson on Route 66. He was not well-off but had a real charm about him that women could not resist. I fell for it, hook, line and sinker, myself, without even a thought, agreeing to sleep with him then return to LA as his girlfriend. I should have realized then that this was temporary insanity; he was a seasoned womanizer, but I was desperately lonely by now and needed a change. The money and business success had not produced the happiness I imagined it would. So, off I went back to America as the maid of honour and my friend got married on a hot sunny day, in LA.

After a long fun day, some amazing champagne, a great toast to the bride from me and some very good long lines of cocaine, the best man, the Mexican brother, invited me to Vegas on the back of his Harley to get married by an Elvis lookalike, in a drive through chapel. Honestly, it sounds ridiculous when I think back but this is exactly how it happened and I just went along with it, without thought, throwing all caution to the wind. The long ride through the night, in the brutal heat of the desert, wearing a crash helmet, having never been on a motorbike before, was a definite first that I will *never* repeat.

To cut this long story short, we got married by the Elvis lookalike, got high as kites to celebrate, gambled till six a.m.

then fell into the large bed in a huge suite at the Bellagio hotel, surrounded by dollar bills, exhausted. What a trip. What an experience. What madness. This was LA LA land remember, where dreams come true, and anything goes. I wanted a change of scenery more than you could ever imagine. I wanted to stop the merry-go-round, get off and relax in the sunshine with my new husband and finally enjoy my hard-earned money.

So, without a thought, I sold my homes, gave my share of the business to my partner, put all my money in the stock market and packed up to move to LA and live happily ever after. By now, my family had got so used to my crazy antics, they just took it all in their stride and were excited to come visit for holidays and a bit of excitement.

Three months after moving into a house in Manhattan beach, by the beautiful ocean, the stock market brutally crashed overnight, my shares dwindled to nothing within days, and I found myself owing the bank money. The dot com bubble burst, as the city and Wall Street suffered an almost 77 percent drop, resulting in a loss of billions of dollars. The big bad bubble also caused many internet companies to go bust and my stocks happened to fall into this category. Overnight, pretty much, I was broke, broken, married to someone I hardly knew, with a friend who was drinking more than ever, to soothe her own pain.

They say what doesn't kill you, makes you stronger but at this point, I just wanted to kill myself and did not feel stronger. The shame and embarrassment, of such an almighty crash from grace, sent me downhill faster than a fox chasing a rabbit. I was devastated, unable for weeks to admit to myself, let alone my new husband, who by now was not as attractive and attentive as he was when I had money, that I was to blame. Greed, illusion, medicating, insanity, and reckless abandonment of any personal responsibility was all I had left to show for years of climbing out of poverty, to reach the top of the world. So, you can see here, I do have a degree from the university of life, making me an expert in mistakes.

After the husband left to live with a new woman and my friend battled to sort out her own situation, I was alone for a week in the house with only my thoughts to keep me company. I got call to tell me that my mother had died in hospital, an alcoholic. I had been back a few times before the crash to see my family and visit her. She was a widow in an old people's home, drinking herself to death. This made me so sad; I could hardly stand it.

Obviously at this stage, I had just lost everything, so couldn't afford to go back for her funeral. Plus, I had so much to deal with in my mind, I just couldn't face them or their questions. It would have taken me down further than I already found myself. As huge waves of anxiety crashed into my mind, dark clouds of depression followed. I couldn't breathe, I couldn't sleep. I just felt so alone, so ashamed, so sad and so empty. I tried drinking some tequila the ex-husband left behind, to ease my pain. I went for long walks on the beach to clear my head. I smoked the last of the pot I had grown in the back garden, but nothing shifted the darkness. Eventually, the storm inside was so violent and out-of-control, after drinking the rest of the tequila and holding a bottle of strong painkillers, I contemplated suicide. My only way out of the dark and my pain.

I took some pills and drank more, until I finally collapsed, waking up the next morning, happier than I had been for a long while. I was alive, grateful, and determined to never consider such a dangerous thing, ever again. I had reached the bottom. Well, at least that is what I thought, but unbeknownst to me, I had more falling to come.

My friend and myself both got divorced from what became known as our jailers and moved in together in a small, rented house away from the beach, where it was much cheaper. I had collected many expensive designer bags and fancy designer clothes, expensive jewellery, paintings, furniture, and other nice things money can buy, which selling at a loss, helped us survive for a few years. We did some crazy things and got involved in some mad LA antics, drinking ourselves into oblivion, to hide the pain and help navigate the slippery slope to the bottom, once again.

As the money began to run out and life in LA was not going so well. I had been bleeding for months but without medical insurance, there was no way I could pay see a doctor. I just kept pushing it all to the back of my mind, praying like mad, to something in the sky to step in and provide the miracle I so desperately needed.

Of course, no one was listening and then one day, without warning, I collapsed from a cardiac arrest. I was rushed to the local hospital, where they are forced to see you in an emergency. Then you pay later once they have saved your life. It turned out I had an eight-pound fibroid, the size of a football, in my uterus and my blood count had drooped so low, my system began to fail, causing the cardiac arrest. I was dying and needed blood transfusions and an emergency hysterectomy, to save my life. I can imagine right now you are thinking to yourself: OMG how did she allow this to happen, stupid idiot?

And all I can say is, you would be right, except for the fact, when you are focusing only on survival, drinking too much and have a huge ego, you still believe you are invincible and someone or something else, will save the day. By never really looking at the trail of devastation, the mistakes, the greed, the mayhem, behind the masks, the lies, and the illusions, what do you end up with? I guess, with exactly what you deserve.

With no medical insurance, after three blood transfusions that failed, in intensive care, I died for a few minutes, left my physical body, and watched myself from above, in the bed with white sheets, covered in blood.

I had a near death experience, which was clear, powerful and, in a funny way, gave me extraordinary peace for just a few moments. It was over. Finally, I had reached the very bottom, of the top of the world.

It turned out, after the hospital team got me back from the brink, with more blood transfusions, I was stable but needed an urgent hysterectomy to remove the monster fibroid, otherwise, I would be a goner for good. I was given tablets to stop the bleeding and sent home, after a few days recovering, with a massive bill I could not pay. I had agreed to travel back to the UK for free medical help on the NHS with my new nurse and friend, once we could find a way to pay for the air tickets, pack up the house and get the hell out of there for good.

For weeks, we struggled to eat, let alone find money for air tickets. I tried to explain to my family and my old rich friends what had happened, but I was too ashamed and embarrassed to be fully honest about my tragic situation. I had terrible status anxiety and just couldn't cope with the idea of being poor and stupid. Be careful of who you hurt and how you treat people on the way up because it does really influence what happens on the way back down.

The landlord repossessed the rented house and threw us out once he realized the severity of the situation, which was brutal and unexpected. You probably have no idea what it is like in the US, when you are a foreigner, without a dime; it truly makes you grateful for all the help offered here in the UK. I begged my ex-business partner to help by sending us two tickets home, so I could get the lifesaving surgery I desperately needed and start to recover. He was traveling but agreed to help when he returned, in two weeks. This left us with a huge dilemma. We were homeless, broke, and desperate, with nowhere to turn and nothing to medicate with, let alone eat.

After visiting the local church, somewhere we had never visited before, the nice kind chaplain suggested we go to a homeless shelter in Compton. The worst, most dangerous part of LA. It was connected to the church, and he believed we would be safe and looked after, until the tickets arrived. Two long weeks in a homeless shelter with no money, pride, or possessions was probably the worst scenario to have to contemplate but as it happened, it turned out to be very enlightening. There were problems at first with all the men in the shelter, druggies, drunks, gang members and potential murderers, sniffing around, intimidating, and watching us like hawks on acid.

I was pushed down on my mattress on the floor one evening when we first arrived, by a Latino thug with a knife at my throat but managed to talk my way out of his anger and change the dynamics. I just told him to just slit my throat and put me out of my misery. I was dying anyway, so had nothing to live for.

Miraculously, he listened to my story and then spent the rest of the time, guarding and protecting us like his own children. You never really know what is around the corner in life. Who would have ever imagined you could one minute be at the top of the world and, the next, right at the bottom?

Returning to the UK, with its arms wide open, was such a miracle and my family stepped up to the plate and helped us beyond belief, something for which I will be eternally grateful. I had the lifesaving surgery on the NHS I needed and within six months, things began to look so much better. We found a small, rented cottage, signed on the dole, got a small business grant, then stated a new small ethical fashion company. My friend was still drinking but I had given up every vice imaginable, including sex, alcohol, meat, dairy, shopping, smoking, and lying, primarily because I couldn't afford any of it.

I began working on helping my friend get sober and deal with her own demons. In LA during my crash, after my attempted suicide, I began reading books about self-analysis by Carl Jung and it truly made sense to me. It helped me with self-reflection, understanding more about my mind, my neurosis, my mistakes, and my past. I knew I could make a comeback in business, bigger and better than before. I also knew instinctively, after such huge life lessons, I had to find my purpose to keep me grounded and give back, not always take. I became a free life coach, funded by my new business, and started working with the homeless and addicted in my spare time. It was fascinating and challenging but I loved it and it helped me recover myself.

I had this degree from the university of life, which truly helped me to connect and empathise with my patients, who could never afford to pay for therapy or help. My friend began to travel backwards over time to examine the wreckage of her own life, with my help. She had been drunk for most of it, to help medicate the pain of a difficult childhood. It took many years but after unscrambling the unconscious in her mind, today she is cured and on the journey to her better, higher self without the crutch of alcohol. It's fantastic.

We survived hell together and are here today, working hard on our ethical business and building something to be proud of. So, you never know what will happen in your life, unless you are travelling the right path for you. You find the right path, through removing your layers, masks, and unconscious beliefs, often inherited, to take a long hard look behind what it is that is leaving you unhappy, making continued mistakes.

Your own life may feel important to you, but does it make you happy? Is there meaning to life? The brutal answer is, no, there is no meaning to life, unless you find your true purpose for being here. You must believe that purpose and that your energy will leave your body more enlightened than it arrived. You must never die or let it become trapped again. You can hide behind the comfort blanket of religion and believe in a God you have no objective evidence exists, other than what you read about it in a book, and that's okay. The earth and the sun will eventually be destroyed, especially the way humans carry on and the universe will also eventually end. A wider interpretation, called the many worlds hypothesis, claims that every time you decide something new, the universe replicates itself. You enter one universe and an alternative you enter the other.

If this is true, your universe is created by the choices *you* make and this is the explanation I have concluded myself, about the meaning of my own life. There are many dimensions. Life and substance are just ideas. Life is energy that propels all our actions. Most of us believe the meaning of life is to find happiness and fulfilment. Others believe the meaning of life comes from a higher purpose, to make the world a better place. Still others believe the meaning of life is to just experience, a live and let live existence, often inherited from someone else's hopes and dreams. But I say, no matter what you believe, make it your absolute intention from now on, to believe only in yourself because this is where your power is.

So that's me in a nutshell, warts, and all. Hopefully, for many of you, my journey will be far worse than yours. I survived to tell this tale, a much better human being because of it. I am still happy today, without any addictions or vices. I am loving my life more than ever. I always look for opportunities to grow further and never just sit back on my laurels. I want to make changes in the bigger picture and won't give up the fight to remind every single person I meet life is so unexplained but so exciting, once you get the hang of why you are here.

To conclude this journey we have travelled together, I am going to now ask you the question. What is the meaning of your own life?

When you really think deeply about this question, looking beyond materialism, purpose, religion, ego, and the life template, what everyone else does, you conclude, it's about your own story. We are all part of an infinite energy source. If energy can never be destroyed, then it is also true, we cannot be destroyed either. Of course, your body eventually dies but your energy does not, so it must go somewhere. Everything that comes into your life, you are attracting through this infinite energy source. Everything you are thinking in your mind, you are attracting back into your life. With all this in mind, we must begin to question what story we are writing ourselves, to leave behind, as a memory because that is all we will be, a memory.

Today after my own extraordinary life story, still not finished, I have concluded, the meaning of life is a collective thing and not just about me. If we all did something good to save the planet, imagine how powerful this collective energy would be. This is the true meaning of purpose and of your life, to do something good for the world. If we all did this, anything would be possible.

But sadly, it is not because as human beings we prefer to fight, have opinions, and believe we are always right. We believe money buys happiness and meaning. We believe love from another person will bring happiness and meaning. We believe, if only we had what everyone else had, we would be happier with meaning. Happiness, just like meaning, is a concept designed by Man in the materialistic world.

Your life may have turned into an accident because you didn't follow your own footprints in the sand. You were potentially led down the wrong path by someone else. You potentially inherited baggage, ideas, opinions, and patterns from someone else's life story. But you, your own energy, is never an accident. Whatever exists in your mind, exists in your life. Unless you change your mind and your thinking, nothing will ever change. It's common sense.

Start thinking, from today, more about your own life story, not just as the memories you leave behind for others but as an experience in the here and now. Rewrite the text by rewiring your thoughts. If you think you are depressed, unhappy, unfulfilled, ask yourself why you think this and what evidence do you have to back it up?

If it is because everything has gone wrong and now you cannot find your way out of the darkness, seek some light. If you believe you are useless, then ask yourself, who told you this? If it turns out to be that cruel stupid critic in your head, take away the power by recognising, this is *not* your voice, then silence it by *not* believing what it is telling you. Your fearful thoughts must now go.

If you are still allowing your fearful thoughts to keep you stuck in that swamp, ask yourself what it is you are afraid of and you will soon conclude, it is nothing to do with fear. It is to do with anxiety, potentially passed on to you as a child or through early life, from the people who cared for you or the circumstances you experienced in the past. If you are now a powerful energy, that can *never* be destroyed, then stop letting the thoughts in your mind, that don't belong to you, become the reason you believe you have no meaning.

It's not easy, but please always remember, every thought in your mind is a real thing and what you put out there, you will always receive back. If the thoughts you have are not real, then what you get back will not be real either.

You have all the power within you to change the ending of this story, your story, regardless of what has happened to you. You own the pen, the paper, and the power to become whatever you desire. You must just believe in yourself, and no one else. Changing anything is never easy because, without clarity, desire, and a good kick up the backside, we remain convinced we are just here for a good time and not a long time. You can never change what has happened in the past, but you can learn to let it go, then you might begin to understand what having a good time really means. The next time you run into conflict in your life, do yourself a favor and look within first for the answer. It is never outside forces that make us necessarily feel something. It is always our irrational interpretation through what we tell ourselves that creates emotional internal turmoil.

The key to balanced mental health is restoring your clean energy throughout your multidimensional body parts (mental, physical, emotional, and spiritual) of your consciousness.

Talking to yourself is never a sign of madness. In fact, you are mad if you never talk to yourself. It is never a sign of poor mental health either. It is normal and a very useful part of self-analysis or self-therapy. We will often find ourselves chatting to ourselves in our minds, usually about making choices. Shall I? Will I? Why did I? I wish I hadn't, etc. Self-talk is good, if it is *you* consciously talking back to *you* and never negative untruths, triggered by stress or anxiety. While you cannot always prevent certain emotions, being mindful can help you manage them. By replacing negative thoughts with more helpful ones, eventually your old habits die and are then replaced by new ones. You are freed from your fear and those heavy chains of anxiety can no longer strangle the strong, authentic, operating person you were born to be.

Goodbye and good luck. And remember, you can always think about hypothetical situations without having to picture yourself in them.